# Fairest Lord Jesus

# Fairest Lord Jesus

Meditations on the Gospels for the Poor in Spirit
and the Contrite Heart

BENJAMIN W. FARLEY

WIPF & STOCK · Eugene, Oregon

FAIREST LORD JESUS
Meditations on the Gospels for the Poor in Spirit and the Contrite Heart

Wipf & Stock
An Imprint of Wipf and Stock Publishers
199 W. 8th Ave., Suite 3
Eugene, OR 97401
www.wipfandstock.com

ISBN 13: 978-1-62032-952-8
Manufactured in the U.S.A.

*Dedicated to*
*Robert Thornton Henderson*

*In Memory of*
*André de Robert*

# Contents

# Preface

THE MEDITATIONS IN THIS little book were written in a period of personal and spiritual duress. Such are common to life. They constitute part of life's journey and our growth in faith. Even the author of Ecclesiastes had his bad days and discouraging moments. "Vanity of vanities, all is vanity!" he wrote. As much as that is true, however, we know that "the sun also rises" and that underneath are God's everlasting arms. It is just that in the process of our sojourning, there are lows and highs that await us along the way.

Sometimes our lows border on despair. One thinks of the young Werther's universal lament when his love for Charlotte appeared dashed and his future glum: "All men are disappointed in their hopes, and deceived in their expectations," he wrote.[1] Still, life is good and filled with exciting surprises. Most of us fall in love and discover opportunities that enrich and fulfill our efforts. As the Psalmist declared so many years ago: "Oh, give thanks to the LORD, for He is good! For His mercy endures forever." [Ps 118:1 KJV]

In truth, we do experience valleys of depression. Our age of instant gratification and our culture's slide into personal and national disparagement has taken its toll on the soul. That so many people suffer from a profound range of multiple personality disorders is equally daunting. The ills of time seep into our consciences and threaten to overwhelm us. We need God's presence. We need those prolonged moments of silence with God in the presence of his Son, undergirded by that ancient story of faithfulness and redemption that the Holy Scriptures proclaim. Where to go to discover anew the roots of our faith if not the Gospels' Son of Galilee? In

1. Goethe, The *Sorrows of Werther*, Dodge Publishing Co. New York, p. 193.

him we find not only consolation for ourselves and our own sorrows and misgivings, but the secret that Christianity's vast host of saints before us have discovered long ago: that in giving we receive, in consoling others we ourselves become consoled, and in loving others become whole.

One further note. From time to time I mention André de Robert and the Centre de Villemétrie. De Robert was the director of a French Protestant Monastery near Paris, which was developed and funded by friends of the French Reformed Church. De Robert was the remarkable figure who directed this *équipe* as it was known—a brotherhood of young men who assisted de Robert and his ministry of *engagement*. On weekends, Christian and secular friends alike would come from Paris to stay with the community and renew their commitments to faith in the midst of secular demands. De Robert was eloquent, quiet, inclusive, an admirer of Rudolf Bultmann's understanding of Jesus, and as saintly a man as I have ever known. He embodied Christ's spirit, Christ's openness and patience, and Christ's love for all. In so many ways, he was as perfect a human incarnation of Jesus' kindness, as one can possibly know.

And so I offer these meditations in the hope that they may encourage and speak to the reader, as in the process of writing them Christ has comforted and ministered to me.

# 1

## Jesus Alone

After saying farewell to them, he went up to the mountain to pray.
When evening came ... he was alone. (Mark 6:46–47)

EVEN JESUS SOUGHT GOD, though God was incarnate in his heart.
True, he had not counted equality with God a thing to be grasped
but had emptied himself (Phil 2:6–7); still he longed for his Father.
Surely we are no different in our longing for God who is engraved
in our hearts, too (Gen 1:27). Indeed, God, whose presence we
long for, is everywhere. God is at the center of the universe as well
as at its circumference. If we ascend to heaven, God is there. If we
make our bed in Sheol, behold, God is there (Ps 139). God is closer
to us than we are to the mystery of our own being. Still, the text
says that Jesus wanted to be with God; that he wanted to be "alone."
There in the sphere of his aloneness, he knew God awaited him.
But first he had to say "farewell" to his disciples to be alone.

We too have to break away at times to be alone, to be by ourselves, where God meets us on his own terms, alone. Ours is a time
of distraction. Of cravings and desires. Of restless longings and un-
ending activity. Can we break from all that long enough to be alone?

In the Greek language, the text for "alone" is *kat' idian*. It
means to be "by oneself," in the stillness of the self, which is so hard

to achieve. A self, alone, neither preoccupied with itself or its sorrows, is difficult to enter; yet it is not impossible. To transcend one's "default," as philosophers express it, is possible.

We in the West have not learned to enter the self as successfully as those in the East. The East has practiced it longer. The Buddha, we are told, sat under a bo tree for forty-nine days before he encountered the depths of the self, where he met himself, if not the mystery we call "God." Theravada Buddhists prefer to explain it as his "Enlightenment," or as the Buddha's "Awakening," as they do not embrace belief in a personal deity. Nonetheless, his "Awakening" was unto *Something* far greater than his personal ego, since the enlightenment he experienced filled him with compassion and insight.

A Jewish mother once put it to me this way: "Do you have to mention God's name for God to be present?" I answered, "No. No more than a child has to cry, 'Mama,' for his mother to rush to his side to kiss away his tears." Her husband, who had lost his family during the Holocaust, refused to allow God's name to be mentioned in his house. He carried that pain, his default all his life. Nevertheless, his wife believed that God was present; thus she would whisper his Name in silence on Friday evenings as she lit the Sabbath candles.

It is good to be alone, alone with the self and alone with God. It is Jesus who set the example when he went up that evening to the mountain to pray.

∼∼∼

When evening came . . . he was alone. (Mark 6:47)

There is something about the evening that invites the self, or the soul, to seek solitude. Perhaps God made it that way, since He foresaw how fraught with worry, or heavy with sorrow, a heart can become by evening. Not that every evening brings a litany of the day's misgivings and woes. It can also bring joy, satisfaction, a sense of accomplishment and pride. "Well done thy good and faithful servant," said Jesus (Matt 25:21). Still, the evening is different. It is special. Remember that God made both day and night, morning and evening, each with its realm of joys and possibilities.

"And there was evening . . ." (Gen 1:5, 8, 13, etc.). And so that evening Jesus sought to be alone. He sought to be with God. It had been a long day. From a basket of five loaves and two fishes, he had fed five thousand. Now it was time to retire. He sent his disciples away. He would meet them in Bethsaida. But just then he needed to be alone, by himself, with the Father. We do not know what he prayed. The hour was late. He had broken bread, he had set the fish before the multitude, and all had eaten before going home. Now it was evening, and he hungered for more than bread, for more than fish. He hungered for God, for the Father in his heart, and for the rest that evening brings.

God gives us the evening as a gift. It is a time for reflection and contemplation, a time for family and friends about the table. Jesus used the evenings for both. His Last Supper was in the evening. His meal with Simon the Pharisee and the girl who wept at his feet, who kissed them with her lips and wiped them with her hair, occurred in the evening. She too hungered for God, to be near God, there at the feet of Jesus. Hers was a self, immersed in the Self of God, a self come home, a self that experienced the healing transcendence above her shame and default.

We too need such evenings. We need them for the soul to find itself again, for the soul to be alone with God, even to be alone with itself. There, in the sphere of genuine self-aloneness, the soul comes before God, who restores and comforts it, beside the still waters of hope.

~~~

Then Jesus was led up by the Spirit into the wilderness . . . (Matt 4:1)

For forty days and forty nights Jesus was alone. "Tempted by the devil," says Matthew. The descent into the self brings us not only into nearness with God but closeness with the dark side of the self. To their profound remorse, Adam and Eve stumbled into their darkness in the cool of the Garden the evening God came to them after their fall. They ran and hid from God, for they were ashamed.

Jesus stared into the pit of his own humanity to face the darkness that lurked there. And it was waiting for him, to lure him away from his closeness to God. All he had to do was to say, "Yes." The temptation was real, present, sweeter than the taste of honey and as mellow as the nectar of gods. Popularity and power, enrobed in majesty, were there for his taking. Jesus said, "No!"

The psychoanalyst Alfred Adler was no stranger to the truth about the dark side. He listed four mistaken goals we are tempted to pursue: attention, power, revenge, and inadequacy. Jesus faced them, ran them through the channels of his heart, and turned away from each. "Man does not live by bread alone." "Thou shalt not tempt the LORD thy God." "Worship the LORD thy God and serve him only."

Carl Jung well understood the power of the inner demonic and the darkness that a repressed unconscious can produce. No personality can achieve integration or know itself, until the prison house of the collective unconscious is allowed to ascend into consciousness. Then and only then can the archetypes of what is fearful and twisted, of what is terrifying and oneiric, become acknowledged, understood, and released. Time and again, Jesus would exorcise these hidden demons in order to set troubled souls free.

After his temptation, "angels came and ministered to him," says Matthew. So it is when we acknowledge the demonic within, let it speak its mind, listen to its plea, but then let it slip away. Then the ministering angels of wholeness come to mend and repair the battered heart. If we are willing to confront the demonic, to allow the Spirit of God to expose it for what it is, and to accept the repressed truth about ourselves, then we too can experience renewal of soul.

≈≈≈

"Here is my servant, whom I have chosen, my beloved,
with whom my soul is well pleased." (Matt 12:18)

The speaker is God. Even God refers to his own soul and how much his soul loves the Son. Jesus had withdrawn in this text. The word is "departed" (Matt 12:15). His healing of a man with a withered hand had angered the Pharisees, since Jesus had healed him on the

Sabbath. Jesus "departed" the place, as he didn't want to make a scene. He didn't even want the crowd "to make him known" (Matt 12:15). He just wanted to be himself and do what God had sent him to do. And God loved him for that. It made God's own being "pleased." To capture that, Matthew used the phrase é *psyché mou*—"my soul." It is God's soul that is pleased.

The Gospels rarely employ the word *psyché* to speak of the soul. In the Hebrew the word is *nephesh*—"a living being." That is what happened to humankind when God breathed his breath, his *ru-ah*, into the wet, nutrient-rich soil of creation. From that holy and wondrous mix, God formed humankind in his image and likeness.

That makes the soul—the *nephesh* of divine breath and alluvial dust—unique. Little wonder that we desire to be alone with God, where once again we long for the Creator to scoop us up into the palm of his hand that he might breathe his love and confidence anew into our hearts. What is the soul, if we might ask? Is it not the presence of God, the very awareness of God within ourselves? That is why, when we are truly alone, we sense his immanence. It is the temple in which God descends to us: his mercy seat in our hearts.

≈≈≈

Six days later, Jesus took with him Peter and James and John,
and led them up a high mountain apart [*kat' idian*], by themselves.
(Mark 9:2)

Once again we meet the phrase *kat' idian*, the *logoi* that means "apart," "alone," "by oneself" (*monous* in Greek). Six days earlier they had perambulated about the villages of Caesarea Philippi. There Jesus had questioned them, "Who do men say that I am?" After listening to their varied replies, he asked anew, "But who do you say that I am?" Not knowing how else to respond, Peter blurted, "Thou art the Christ! The Anointed One!"

They were alone then. Now even more so! If the least kernel of the historical clings to the threads of this story, it lies in the likelihood that Jesus had led them up Mt. Hermon. Sun-clad, even throughout the hottest days of summer, its snow-blinding glare numbed their senses and transfixed them with its glowing aura. Jesus' garments blazed white with fire. The crackling ice, trickling and trembling in the sun, added its lyrical tone to the spectral epiphany that swept over them. They had ascended into the realm of the holy without comprehending what had happened. They were unprepared. Yet their deepest instincts grasped the significance of the moment. "It is good to be here!" Peter mumbled amid the misty updrafts and sun-bright clouds.

Yes, it was good to be there, to be in the presence of the holy, where light and cloud, ice and sun, began to disclose the splendor of the soul's encounter with God. We too require such magical moments, or the heights of a *kat' idian*, or retirement to a lonely place, away from the clamor of the mundane. Reflection, contemplation, and listening to the voice within have the potential of drawing us closer to the possibility of meeting God—though the God we meet there must not be confused with the self. The text adds that Moses and Elijah appeared to accompany Jesus. Standing in the mist, both Old Testament figures wavered before the disciples. The solemn patriarchs seemed lost themselves in silent dialogue with their LORD. They too had known the silence of aloneness, the mystery of *kat' idian* in their respective time and place. Moses, stumbling into the wadi where fire dazzled in a bush that remained unburned! Elijah, in flight from Ahab, the Israelite king, crouching in a cave, suddenly sensing the presence of God in the still small voice that whispered outside the entrance!

It is good to seek, if not even stumble from time to time, into the shadow of the *kat' idian*. Once, while hiking about Inscription Rock, remote in the desert near Grant, New Mexico, I found myself descending a path that opened into a bright glade. The red and yellow hues of the canyon's walls glowed in the sun's soft glory. And, there, in the center of the glade, a tall green juniper, stretching its branches toward the blue sky, stood ablaze in the sunlight. A silence fell about the place—a hush that could be felt, a stillness that shimmered in the radiant light. I stopped and stared. I was one with Moses and Elijah, transfigured with Jesus and the disciples. I wanted to stay, to indulge the epiphany as long as possible. But, just as suddenly, the phenomenon slipped away. Nonetheless, the shadow of the Almighty accompanied me all the way out and buoyed my soul during the long drive back to Albuquerque. I knew I had been in the presence of God, or, if not God, in the presence of something so incarnated in my soul that only the name of God could do justice to the mystery and joyful nuances it unleashed within.

Perhaps the brain has evolved in such a way that it can never lose its capacity to find refuge in the depths of itself, where the wonder and glory of the memory of God resides.

≈≈≈

"The hour is coming ... when you will be scattered ... and you will
leave me alone [*ta 'ida*]. Yet I am not alone [*monos*] because the
Father is with me." (John 16:32)

The difference between being alone and being lonely, between "aloneness" and "loneliness," is well known. The former makes possible the phenomena of reflection and contemplation, memory and soul searching, meditation and openness to self and God. The latter seeps into the self and fills it with dejection, even despair. It is not uncommon for the lonely to experience feelings of abandonment, of low esteem, and the temptation to seek succor in self-pity. "O God, please pity me!" Even the Israelites, in their time of exile, succumbed to self-pity.

> By the rivers of Babylon—
> there we sat down and there we wept ...
> On the willows there we hung our harps ...
> How could we sing the LORD's song in a foreign land?
> (Ps 137:1–2, 4)

Aristotle considered philosophical contemplation the highest goal a human life could attain. In his mind, to contemplate one's highest *teleos*, or highest purpose, edifies the mind and renews one's vision and courage. Such reflection encourages transcendence. For Jesus, it lifted his spirit to God, to "the Father," with whom his heart was infinitely united. Nonetheless, an aloneness that fails to transcend itself can collapse into the loneliness of helplessness and remorse.

> My soul is consumed with longing . . .
> My soul clings to the dust . . .
> My soul melts away with sorrow.
> (Ps 119: 20, 25, 28)

Concomitantly, a loneliness that acknowledges its isolation and inescapable despair, and chooses to exercise what Paul Tillich called "the courage to be," can become reunited with its larger self, which God indwells. "Where can I go from your spirit? Where can I flee from your presence?" (Ps 139:7).

Plainly stated, we are never far from God. The void into which we sometimes fall is equally home to the steps of heaven that ascend to the Father again. The miracle of the self, the soul, created in the image of God, is what makes this possible.

~~~

In the morning, while it was still very dark, he got up and went out to a deserted place [*eis érémon topon*], and there he prayed. (Mark 1:35)

While working one summer on an Israeli kibbutz, our party of youths was given a tour of the Galilee. We arrived before dawn, while the night was still nigh. Beyond the hills to the east, toward the Golan Heights, the opaque dome of the sky stared down in silent darkness. We climbed a hill that overlooked the sea. We each sought a quiet place, an *érémon topon* of our own, to await the rising sun and commune with our soul and God. Below us the lake reflected the soft gray wonder of the clouds high over the slumbering sea. Then dawn broke faintly over the eastern hills. It was a time of long ago, in a *topon* of long ago, before the region erupted into decades of unmitigated sorrow. I can still see the lake, semi-dark in the last throes of night, and feel the silence that lifted the soul both up and within to wait before God, to see what Jesus must have seen, and ponder what that self-emptying Galilean must have thought.

Farther to the east, long before Jesus was born, human hearts had been doing the same. In Sumer and Babylon, they greeted

Ishtar, the Morning Star, with a hope and hunger that Jesus would have recognized and blessed as a cry for God. In the Rig Veda, it is the goddess Dawn that fills her devotees' hearts with joy and promise, as her aura sends her sister, Night, fleeing into the *topon* where darkness reigns.

Both cultures prized the silence of the morning, with its freshening rays of cleansing light—the harbinger of a new day. To be still and know that God is nigh fills the soul with redemption and renewal. Yesterday is gone, like a thief in the night. The dawn represents renewal. "As far as the east is from the west, so far he removes our transgressions from us" (Ps 103:12).

The "deserted place" refers to our hearts, to our souls, when we finally empty them of self-pretension, pride, and insatiable lusts, and in their place make room for God. As the Psalmist knew and Jesus embraced, "When I was brought low, he saved me" (Ps 116:6).

∾∾∾

"Now my soul [*psyché*] is troubled ..." (John 12:27)

The Greek text's phrase is unique: é *psyché mou*—"the soul of me," or "my soul." It may strike us as strange to think of Jesus as having a troubled soul. In theological language, he is the Second Person of the Trinity. Does each member of the Trinity have a separate soul? One for the Father, one for the Son, and one for the Holy Ghost? Augustine warns us that once we begin to think in terms of three we fragment the mystery of God. God is One, but in his holy mystery, God manifests himself to us in many ways. The credo of Father, Son, and Holy Ghost provides us with a language that enables us to acknowledge God's eternal self-manifestation. As Creator, Redeemer, and Holy Spirit, God is ever present to renew, reclaim, and draw us to himself. Only the soul of God could be that big.

Jesus' soul was troubled. He suspected what lay ahead, both for himself and his disciples. His was an anxiety unto death, for himself and each of them. The final hour was near. John saw it in retrospect. Jesus saw it as a prospect. Either way, it troubled Jesus' soul. What would be the larger meaning of his life? As a Galilean, he could not have known. As the Son of Man, he could only project. "Who do men say that I am?" "What do you say?"

To reflect on the mystery of our own being is always troubling. As Tolstoy's Ivan Ilych was forced to put it, "What if all that I have done is wrong and my life cannot be rectified?" It is the cry of every soul: "What if all that I have lived for is wrong and cannot be rectified? Is the larger meaning of my life defined by my default? Can it ever be redeemed? Can I ever be lifted above my past? Am I condemned to carry it like an albatross about my neck till the day I die? Can I ever be more than my pride, my foolishness, and my past have condemned me to be?" It is a genuine cry. "Have I no future, God? Have I only my past that will mar every crevice of my future?"

Listen to Jesus' answer: "Now my soul is troubled. And what should I say—'Father, save me from this hour'? No, it is for this reason that I have come to this hour" (John 12:27). Is it not possible that the troubling hour is the hour in which the soul most discovers the truth about itself? A finite, broken, and contrite heart God will not despise (Ps 51). Is that why John refers to this hour as the hour of Jesus' "glorification"? The glorification of a soul set free? Is that not the message we too need to hear? Our soul is most glorified when we are most honest with ourselves. Letting our troubled soul acknowledge its troubled condition brings us face to face with ourselves and with the mystery of God. To be set free from that "trouble" is to be "glorified," as our past is taken up into God's heart and his heart flows back into ours.

≈≈≈

"I am forgetting myself, and my mind is reeling." (Bhagavad Gita 1:30)

The West is not the only culture whose religious people have descended into the troubled self. The Hindu scriptures of the Bhagavad Gita attest to the universal presence of the troubled soul. The above quotation comes from the lips of the young prince Arjuna. He is mounted on his chariot, dressed in the armor of war; his steeds thundering toward the armies of his own kin, a battle between kingdoms. "I do not see what any good can come from this," he whispers to Lord Krishna, who rides incarnate beside him. Lord

Krishna is the god Vishnu in human form; Vishnu is the redeemer god of India, the god of wisdom and compassion—the Eastern counterpart to YWHW of the Hebrew Bible.

Lord Krishna listens to the young prince, then replies, "Those who are wise lament neither for the living nor the dead. Never was there a time when I did not exist, nor you, nor all these kings; nor in the future shall any of us cease to be" (2:11–12 ).

That may be more than Christianity can embrace. Yet, the universal purport is there. The chariot is the self; the soul, Arjuna; his holy rider, God! On the eve of that epic battle between the Hindu clans whose victory would determine India's fate, the young prince Arjuna could not help but raise the question of the human condition. In his scriptures, he too meets God whom he can never lose, and from whom he can never be separated. Thus, he rides forward, to the sound of celestial conch shells, to fulfill his destiny as a prince. Vishnu has secured his future. Behold, his past is safe in God's hands.

Paul's letter to the Romans sounds a similar chord. "We know that all things work together for good for those who love God, who are called according to his purpose . . . whom he foreknew, . . . whom he predestined, . . . whom he justified, . . . and whom he glorified. What then are we to say? If God is for us, who is against us?" (Rom 8:28–36).

The descent of the troubled soul, as troubling as it may seem, can be the portal for finding God again. Therein lies the possibility of discovering one's authentic self: renewed, redeemed, with a future borne on the wings of God.

~~~

"My soul is grieved, even unto death." (Mark 14:32)

Again the words in Greek are é *psyché mou*—"the soul of me," or "my soul." Interestingly enough, the RSV translates it, "I am deeply grieved, even unto death." Far wiser to stay with the Greek: "My *soul* is grieved, even unto death." The soul's grief, even unto death, plunges the soul into the depths of its finitude. For Jesus, it was the imminent nearness of his own death that caused his soul to grieve.

Still he knew that unless a grain of wheat falls into the earth and dies, it cannot bear fruit. As he explained for his disciples, "Whoever saves his life will lose it, but whoever loses his life for my sake will find it" (Mark 8:35). Jesus knew the self too well not to acknowledge this truth.

The way to renewal is hard. It requires the death of the thwarted soul, of that thwarted self that can't let go of its dark heart. That self must go before the self that God has created us to be can become a reality. This second birth requires the withdrawal of the old self in order for the new self to come into existence. That is so difficult to do. What other self have we known but our old self? How can we simply slough it off? Let it go? Let it die? Will it away, as if we were saying farewell to an old friend!

Even Hinduism speaks of a "twice-born self." Ceremonies are celebrated to acknowledge its birth. A sacred cord is worn across one's shoulder as a sign of one's binding to a new life. Words of truth are whispered into the initiate's ear; they will become the twice-born person's guiding mantra for the rest of his or her life.

Much of Jung's psychology of the balanced self is based on Jesus' principle of *renovatio*. Until our conscious self recognizes its buried self, there can be no wholeness. That old self has to be called up and out and integrated, or even exorcised, if we are to be whole. The collective unconscious or archetypal self must be let out. It requires the "death" of a part of the self to be born again. Letting go of our cherished self, with all its dark and borderline repressed grandiosity, is hardly a childish task. But it is the death of that self that brings new life. Not even Jesus was immune. There can be no new life without letting go of the old one.

Jesus refers to the ordeal as a "cup." "Father, if it be possible, remove this cup from me!" (Mark 14:36). In the end, however, he drank his cup, as did Socrates drink his. There comes a point in life when we either drink our "cup," or clutch the old and keep it brimful with droughts we refuse to give up.

Jesus drank the cup, and at his last supper passed it around for his disciples to drink with him. There is nobleness there for the soul to clasp. A joy that turns sorrow into life! The communion of Christ's heart with ours! The sacrament of oneness with God!

≈≈≈

While it was still dark, Mary Magdalene came to the tomb. (John 21:1)

Even in the darkness, she came to the tomb. Darkness seems to crave darkness, just as misery purportedly loves company. To reflect in darkness, to grieve in darkness, and, when sorrowful, to seek darkness seems to provide a level of comfort for the soul. To be out of view, to remain anonymous, and to be able to contemplate life's deepest disappointments, undetected and detached, provides security and solace for the heart. Like a wounded animal, licking its wounds in the safety and seclusion of its lair, so darkness affords protection and healing for the wounded soul, the uncertain self.

According to John, Mary was shocked to discover that the stone confining Jesus' body had been removed from the tomb. The darkness and sorrow she had brought to the tomb was now exceeded by an even greater darkness and sorrow: "They have taken the LORD out of the tomb, and we do not know where they have laid him" (John 20:2).

We must not be afraid of the darkness within, nor the darkness without. They mask both our fears and the truth about ourselves. We fear that the light will expose us. Nor are we ready to depart from our darkness. It has protected us, concealed our doubts and anxieties, and now we fear what life might require without them. As long as the darkness is there, we feel safe. Better to be fearful and safe than to be pushed into the open, exposed and required to function beyond our inveterate dysfunction. But even the dark is not dark to God. Nor is it beyond God's angels' power to roll the stone away from the tomb within! That is what makes this passage so special. Our darkness is as light to God. Nor can the darkness keep God away. "Rabbouni! Is that you?" (John 21:16.)

≈≈≈

"Be still, and know that I am God!" (Ps 46:10)

As the hour of Jesus' glorification drew near, he set his face toward Gethsemane. He wanted his disciples to wait for him, to watch with him, to remain close by, though he knew he needed to be alone. On his cross, he would recite Psalm 22, if not in its entirety, at least its opening line: "My God, my God, why hast thou forsaken me?" But at Gethsemane, that hour was still a morning's dawn away.

Psalm 46:1 opens with Luther's beloved lines: "God is our refuge and strength." But to draw on God's strength and to enter into God's refuge calls for the heart's preparation. One has to seek the stillness where God may be found to enter into that infinite Calm that awaits us.

Jesus knelt at Gethsemane and emptied himself before God. Three times he implored his Father to remove the cup of his impending cross. Three times in the stillness of that quiet night, he waited for his Father to speak out of his own silence and answer his prayer. As the silence deepened and engulfed him, Jesus accepted his Father's will and drew on the strength of God. "The LORD of hosts is with us; the God of Jacob is our refuge" (Ps 46:11). To be still and know that God is God is to know the God of Jacob, the God of refuge. It was all the refuge that Jesus needed. He rose, awakened his disciples; already the temple guards' torches were in view.

&#x223D;&#x223D;&#x223D;

"My God, my God, why hast thou forsaken me?" (Mark 15:34)

In his daunting classic, *The Gay Science*, Friedrich Nietzsche hurls out a phrase that still torments the soul: "in your loneliest loneliness" (*in deine einsamste Einsamkeit*, par. 341). Only the soul can experience the "loneliest loneliness." Once one's fantasies are stripped away, the soul has to face itself without delusion. It is that moment of moments that cannot be outdistanced. It forces us to come face to face with the self.

Nietzsche calls it the "greatest weight." In his taunting style, he asks:

> What if some day or night a demon were to steal after you into your loneliest loneliness and say to you: "This life as you now live it and have lived it, you will have to live once more and innumerable times and there will be nothing new in it, but every pain and every joy and every thought

and sigh . . . in your life will have to return to you. . . . The eternal hourglass of existence is turned upside down again and again, and you with it, speck of dust!"[1]

"My God, my God!" Jesus cried as he faced his own moment of "greatest weight." Its value is that it plunges us straight into the mystery of God. There we meet God as we are, without the veneer of falsehood, self-deception, or self-righteousness. All that is blown away. "My God, my God! All thy waves and thy billows have gone over me!"

In its context, Nietzsche's "loneliest loneliness" was meant to wrestle with the myth of eternal return. Ancient philosophers reasoned that if there were an infinite number of possibilities but only a finite number of entities, at some point a finite entity's number would come up again. It would come full circle and live its life all over. Nietzsche, however, took the argument a step further. For Nietzsche, every day the cycle of life repeats itself. Every day we are plunged into that loneliest loneliness anew. It will always be that way. Every day we have to face the truth about ourselves. As Nietzsche saw it, that meant having to reaffirm one's existence, in spite of one's inevitable loneliness. It defines us as humans. No one can face it for you; no one can reaffirm your life but you. Jesus understood that. In our loneliest loneliness we come closer to God than at any other moment in our lives. To cry out to God in those moments of reality is to realize that only God can fill the space of abandonment that our loneliness compels us to acknowledge.

As Jesus hung on the cross, Luke tells us that his last words were not "Why hast thou forsaken me?" but "Father, into thy hands I commend my spirit" (Luke 23:46). In the final analysis, Jesus' dying prayer recasts our loneliness as an opportunity for beholding God.

≋≋≋

It was now about noon, and darkness came over the whole land; . . .
while the sun's light failed. (Luke 23:44–45)

The earth shook and the rocks were split. (Matt 27:51)

1. Friedrich Nietzsche, *The Gay Science*, trans. Walter Kaufmann (New York: Vintage, 1974), 273.

Is it scarcely a wonder that the foundations of the earth shook and rocks split at the death of Jesus? Even if Luke and Matthew meant their reports only as metaphor, they could not have selected more appropriate symbols. Sartre devotes an entire volume of his trilogy about World War II to "the death of the soul." In French he entitles the volume *La Mort Dans L'Âme*. Literally, it means "death in the soul," or "the soul's death." Oddly, however, in English the novel was given the title *Troubled Sleep*. In this volume Sartre argues that "men get the war they deserve," and that "Liberty is Terror." In other words, we get the life we deserve and the choice of changing that life is filled with terror. No authentic life is without risk. It is an earth-shattering choice. Terror accompanies our decision to abandon an inauthentic life for a truly authentic life, for which we alone must take responsibility. Darkness comes over the soul's sight; the sun's light fails. What should a soul do? Whoever seeks to save his life will lose it, but whoever loses his life for my sake and the gospel's will save it, said Jesus. Unless you deny yourself and take up your cross, you cannot ascend the heights of liberty.

As that evening came to a close, the women who watched from afar (Luke 23:49) never forgot the failing light, nor the unseen hands that gathered Jesus to the Father's bosom and bore his soul to heaven.

"Surely he was the Son of God," whispered the Centurion (Matt 27:54).

~~~

"Just as Jonah was in the belly of the sea monster for three days and three nights, so also shall the Son of Man be in the belly of the earth."
(Matt 12:40)

"Deep calls to deep at the thunder of thy cataracts; all thy waves and billows have gone over me." (Ps 42:7)

In Hebrew, "sea monster" is *danah*—one word, meaning "fish." All YWHW's waves and billows had gone over Jonah. In terror, the sea-farers had cast him into the wrath of the raging sea. He was running from God, fleeing from his post as YWHW's prophet, YWHW's *nabi*. His task: to proclaim the acceptable year of the LORD. His audience: the sin-hardened and unrighteous fallen of Ninevah. Now in the womb of the great *danah*, he lifted his voice to God: "Out of the belly of Sheol I cried, and you heard my voice. You cast me into the deep; . . . all your waves and billows passed over me. The deep surrounded me, . . . weeds wrapped around my head; . . . yet you brought up my life from the Pit" (Jon 2:1–6).

Why must we go down to the "sea," the biblical pit of a lost and drowning self, before we realize the perilous condition of our souls? It took Jonah three days and three nights, the symbol of death's dark passage from life to limbo, to recognize his flight from reality and YWHW's love. As the sea's depths slowly crushed the great fish's own capacity for life, so Jonah gasped for God's life-giving *ruah* once again. And the God of Israel, who neither slumbers nor sleeps, saw his plight and heard his plea and "lifted" him to life, as he would later lift his own Son, and each of us, to life again, if we but ask.

≈≈≈

"In the belly of the earth." (Matt 12:40)

"Darkness had fallen upon the hill. . . . Huddled in my narrow cave, . . . blackness was wrapped around me. It seemed to cut me off from the outside world. . . . It made me listen to the voices within me." (John Fire Lame Deer)

In his remarkable account of his life as a medicine man, John Fire Lame Deer opens his memoir, *Lame Deer: Seeker of Visions*, with the story of his first vision quest. The young Sioux boy was sixteen. Like his fathers before him, he longed to become a medicine man. But first, however, there were obligations to meet, insight to gain, virtues to prove, resolves to be tested. The required moments in the sweat lodge had cleansed his spirit, tingled his skin, and made his brain feel empty. Perhaps that was good, he thought, for now there was room for new insight and vision. As he crouched in the pit, he could hear the hoof beats of buffalo, the whisper of the wind, songs of birds, the cry of eagles, and the voices of his ancestors. All called him to a new identity, to a life dedicated to serve his people. Voices comforted and challenged him. He was to harm no one, befriend and heal all whom he could, to respect the earth, its creatures, their lives as well as his own. The voice within finally concluded, "A man's life is short. Make yours a worthy one."[2]

Lame Deer goes on to explain that the Sioux believe that "there is something within" that controls one, almost "like a second person." The Sioux word for this person is *nagi*, so similar to the Hebrew word for prophet. It is what other religions mean by "spirit," "soul," or "essence." It cannot be seen, tasted, or touched, but he knew that during those four days and four nights he spent in his vision pit, "it was there inside of me." He felt its power surge through him, preparing him to become a medicine man. "It filled all of me." Then he wept, but his tears were tears of happiness.[3]

2. John Fire, *Lame Deer: Seeker of Visions* (New York: Pocket Books, 1972), 6.

3. Ibid.

# 2

# Jesus as Comforter

"Come unto me, all ye that labour and are heavy laden, and I will give you rest." (Matt 11:28 KJV)

WHEN IT IS ALL said and done, we come to Jesus' sacred place of rest, not only because of our own need, but because he calls us to come. Perhaps we are stunned that he should include us, or humbled that knowing our frame he still opens his heart to us. "*Venite ad me, omnes qui laboratis et onerati estis, et ego reficiam vos*" (Vulgate). "Comfort, O comfort my people, says your God. Speak tenderly to Jerusalem," is the way Second Isaiah phrased it for Judah (Isa 40:1).

"Come unto me, all ye that labor and are heavy laden." You will not find these words in Plato's *Republic*, as brilliant as his city-state of philosopher-kings promised to be. Nor will you will find them in Rousseau's magnificent call to become members of his Social Contract: "Man is born free, and is everywhere in chains." Nor will you hear them in Hamlet's impassioned monologues, nor in Jefferson's Declaration of Independence, nor in the verses of Whitman's poems for the Union fallen, "Come Up from the Field, Father," nor in his sad remembrances of the Confederate dead, "As Toilsome I Wandered Virginia's Woods." Not that any of these writers' prose or eloquence is unworthy of the human condition. Far to the contrary! Socrates, Rousseau, Shakespeare, Jefferson, and Whitman all knew the human condition: that we are born to struggle and sorrow as surely as sparks fly upward! To joy and loss, happiness and despair, passion and tears, bliss and remorse. They are inseparable from our human journey. But so also are peace, consolation, meditation, and God's love. That is why Jesus' tender words comfort our hearts and mend our spirits.

Since his birth, debate has raged over Jesus' holy nature: true man, true God. How can both be? Or was he only a man, like any other man, his conscience caught between God and his neighbors' plight and crushing poverty? Was he a saint or a cynic? A sage or carpenter? The Messiah or only a companion of fishermen? A revolutionary or merely a mendicant? The Son of God or Son of Man? Theological quandaries abound. But what captures the anxious heart is the Gospels' portrayal of Jesus as the mystery of God in humble form: empty of self-advancement, greed, pride, or cloying power. He listened without condemning the broken in spirit; he healed, was gentle, kind, and quick to love. He offered hope to the discouraged and welcomed all who sought him as he was.

How can we not but be drawn to him? For in him we find encouragement again, the renewal of our faith, the will to love, and the power to forgive! O God, fill us with such love again, with such tenderness and care, that we may be gentle and kind, forgiving and inclusive of all thy dear children and humanity everywhere.

≈≈≈

"Take my yoke upon you, and learn from me: for I am gentle and humble in heart, and you will find rest for your souls. For my yoke is easy, and my burden is light." (Matt 11:29)

My mother could never pass a house whose residents were obviously poor without wanting my father to drive her straight home, so she could prepare a box of food and clothing for the family. Like so many men, he urged her to leave well enough alone, but she always managed to coax him to return, whereupon she would place her love gift on the family's doorstep or dilapidated porch. The thought of not helping someone, especially children, was too great a burden for her not to amend. She carried a small silver cross in her purse till the day she died. I never knew it until after her death. I happened to open her purse, and there it was!

Perhaps only a heart that has been comforted can comfort in return. She knew her source of comfort, the gentle yoke of a loving heart that longs to love in turn.

In his book *The Story of San Michele*, the Scandinavian Alex Munthe writes of his many years as a physician in the high societies of Paris, Rome, and Naples. In story after story, he describes what it was like to be a medical doctor in Europe in the late 1870s through the 1920s. Though the affluent and noble-born comprised his patients, much of his labor involved voluntary stints with Catholic hospitals and charities, clinics and direct work among the poor. Not once did he resent the cry of the neglected, the diseased, the ill, and dispossessed. As his narrative unfolds, he reminds us of the one thing he learned over and over again: if you cling to anything you will lose it, but if you give it away, it always comes back. In doing so, he discovered ever and again the secret of joy and happiness, of what truly comforts the human heart. Having been among the wretched, and nurtured by their humility and common grace, he dared to write the following of those who say they care but don't:

> Novel writers, who insist on taking their readers to the slums, seldom go there themselves. Specialists on disease and Death can seldom be persuaded to come with you to the hospital where they have just finished off their heroine. Poets and philosophers, who in sonorous verse and prose hail Death as the Deliverer, often grow pale at the very mention of the name of their best friend. It is an old story.[1]

Jesus reminds us that our souls rest best when we take up his yoke of love and his burden of care for others.

---

1. Alex Munthe, *The Story of San Michele* (New York: E.P. Dutton, 1930), xi.

～～～

And Jesus said to them, "I am the bread of life. He who comes to me
shall never hunger, and he who believes in me shall never thirst."
(John 6:35 KJV)

In the evenings at Villemétrie, we sat in the grand salon and chose
a memory verse for the next day. Each brother was encouraged to
select a passage that most seemed to speak to our collective en-
deavor. After sharing our choices, André would either approve of
one or ask us to vote on the text that most appealed to all. Since we
were reading from Louis Segond's French translation of the Hebrew
and Greek Testaments, I still have all of my stay's memory verses
underlined in ink. How they spoke to our work! Our spirit! Our
life as brothers and novice monks under André's guidance! I still
read them from time to time, drawing as much strength from the
memory of that year's goodness as if André and the *équipe* were still
present with me. The following day we would recite the memory
verse in unison at both morning and evening services in our chapel.
Throughout the day, we would call it to memory wherever we were,
whatever we were doing, as we fulfilled our individual tasks.

Sometimes at the vesper services we chanted passages from
the Psalms. Our voices would unite in *a capella* as we intoned the
Scriptures' sacred words. My favorite was the opening verse of
Psalm 42. In French it went something like this:

*Com-me le cerf alteré a soif de l'eau vivante;*
*Ansi j'ai soif à toi, Seigneur mon Dieu.*

It isn't quite that eloquent in English, but how it tears at our heart:

*As the deer pants for the water brooks,*
*so pants my soul for Thee, O God.*

Life is more than what we eat or drink or wear or under what
roof we lie down at night to sleep. It has to do with the living God
and his Son's presence in our hearts. Then, as tough as life is, "these
things shall be added to you," says Jesus (Matt 6:33).

~·~·~

"The Holy Spirit will come upon you, and the power of the Most High
will overshadow you." (Luke 1:35)

Samuel had observed the young Saul for years. Perhaps he possessed the mettle to rally the Israelites and save them from their
enemies, the Philistines. YWHW's voice in Samuel's soul seemed
to affirm this assessment. So he blessed the son of Benjamin and
prophesied that the Spirit of the LORD would come upon him.
It would possess him and "turn him into a different person." He
would become an ecstatic, like the prophets in the hills, and dance
to flute and tambourine, and God would bless whatever he favored
doing (1 Sam 10:9). And for several years YWHW blessed him.
He was the last great "valiant man" of the Old Testament. But his
glance was backward, his vision anchored in Israel's past. The spirit
that empowered him belonged more to the era of Israel's judges and
warlords than to the future that YWHW foresaw. No one wishes to
fault Samuel or YWHW for Saul's descent into early dementia or
his tragic death on Mt. Gilboa. After all, the Spirit of God solicits
our own cooperation and self-affirmation of his role in our lives. To
veto his voice is a choice that can only result in remorse.

Mary chose to accept the Spirit's role, as defined by Gabriel.
Whatever her future might hold, however wrought with pain and
surprise, worries or wonder she opened her life to the Spirit of the
Most High. She was willing for her ego to be overshadowed by
God's promise.

It is so difficult to let go of the past, let alone an ego that exults
in itself. To cling to its shadows and familiar rounds is so reassuring.
It provides comfort, a savoir-faire that remains within our power to
enact or evoke whenever in doubt or trouble. But the good news
of Gabriel's visitation is that the overshadowing grace of God can
lift us beyond that impasse. Whatever Mary's background, it filled
her soul with magnanimity and rejoicing to say "Yes" to God. It
fulfilled her beyond her highest thoughts. "*Magnificat anima mea
Dominum!*" was her ultimate response (Luke 1:46 Vulgate). It is

worth our own pondering, especially if we hope to become "a different person."

~~~

"For we observed his star at its rising." (Matt 2:3)

"And you, Bethlehem . . . for from you shall come a ruler who is to shepherd my people Israel." (Matt. 2:6)

To the tinkling of the camel bells, the wise men wrapped in their ornate robes followed the star that led them to the town of Bethlehem. The birth of Jesus fills us with its wistful transcendence and star-bright splendor. Behold God, coming down the steps of heaven with a baby in his arms, as Paul Scherer once described it. The Shepherd of Israel, the Everlasting Father, the Prince of Peace had come to his own.

Not only does the story captivate our hearts with its magical sounds and evening stars, but it generates a sense of calm, of unparalleled anticipation of God's arrival in the guise of a baby boy. King of Kings! LORD of Lords. For he has come to comfort his exiles, to bring them home, to raise them to new heights of deliverance and joy.

Herod sought to kill the lad. He wanted peace at any price. He and all Jerusalem were troubled, states Matthew. What troubled them were their own egos, enmeshed in self, pride, their inner darkness, inadequacy, and fear of exposure. It does not have to be that way. When the wise men arrived at the holy site, they were "overwhelmed with joy" and "knelt down" and worshiped him (Matt 2:10–11).

~~~

"Fear not, for I bring you tidings of great joy, . . . for unto you is born this day in the city of David a savior, who is Christ the LORD." (Luke 2:11)

At one time or other, every civilization has longed for the arrival of its Savior. At the time Luke was writing, the Roman Empire had found its savior in Caesar Augustus. In his victory over Mark

Antony, he had rescued the fractured republic from decades of bitter, political turmoil and divisive feuds. Following his "father" Julius Caesar's assassination, the adopted Octavius became *"divi filius,"* or Son of God. In 27 BC he was declared "Augustus," and in AD 14, one month after his death, the senate of Rome declared him "divine." Luke fully grasped Rome's intention, which is why he mentions Augustus in his story of Jesus' birth. It was Luke's way of reminding the soul to render unto Caesar the things that are Caesar's, but unto God the things that are God's: mainly, our hearts to Christ.

King David was a savior for Israel; Asoka for India; Alexander for Macedonia; Constantine for Rome; Charlemagne for Christendom; Washington, Lincoln, and Eisenhower for America, each in his own way and in his own time. Such "grand men," as Hegel calls them, capture the spirit of the time and help launch new eras.

The coastlands await such justice and rejoice in the commonweal it provides (Isa 42:6; 49:6). The soul is no different. It too longs for a *euaggelion* of great joy that can free it from its prison house of despair and doubt. It yearns for a savior who can awaken the soul's need for transformation and renewal. The birth of Jesus as Savior assures us that redemption is possible. Whenever and wherever eternity touches time, a life can be liberated from its broken hopes. "Unto you is born this day in the city of David a Savior." The angels never cease to sing that promise for the heart to hear. But where is the city of David today, if not in your heart and mine? Where is the city of Zion, if not in the depths of the soul? Where is the child of Bethlehem, if not in the cradle of your heart?

∽∽∽

"Blessed be the LORD God of Israel, for he has looked favorably on his people." (Luke 1:68)

Zechariah's *"Benedictus Dominus"* both comforts and prods us. It comforts us with the knowledge that God's heart is moved by the plight of his people. Though we deserve the lives we get—to paraphrase Sartre—God nonetheless cares for his beleaguered offspring. Simultaneously, it prods us because we know that deep down in our hearts our era has turned from God. Since Nietzsche's shocking "death of God" pronouncement of over a hundred and thirty years ago, our modern era has yet to resolve the nihilism Nietzsche foresaw. Against that stark assessment, the New Testament's *Benedictus Dominus* offers an alternative that transcends time. The good news of the gospel remains firm: that God looks favorably upon his own, even if they have strayed like sheep, or wandered off to the prodigal land.

With the birth of John the Baptist, an *événement* occurred, a movement of hope and promise, of expectation and self-examination, that spoke to the underlying uneasiness of a people's dream. Life can be changed; new beginnings are possible; old habits can be cast off. It can happen to you. It can happen to a nation, to an entire generation of moorless youth, of couples and aging populations. Stagnation occurs only when we will it, only when we cease to dream dreams and entertain visions.

The gospel ever remains the gospel: that when we are weak, God is strong; that when we are brought low, God saves us. That a broken and contrite heart God will not despise. That if with all our heart we truly seek him, we will surely find him (1 Chr 28:9). That all who come to him, weak and heavy laden, will find rest unto their souls.

The good news is that we too can sing Zachariah's song. It is meant for us, not just Zachariah. Our hearts can sing it even now.

∼∼∼

Simeon … was righteous and devout,
looking forward to the consolation of Israel (Luke 2:25)

Simeon was in the temple when Mary and Joseph carried the baby Jesus into its sacred area to dedicate their firstborn son to God. As Simeon looked upon the child, a solace beyond comprehension filled his heart. The Greek word for "solace" or "consolation" is *paraklésis*. John's "paraclete" of chapter 16:7 draws from the same source: comforter, advocate, healer, Spirit of the living God!

Luke tells us that Simeon took the child in his arms and blessed him. His inimitable *Nunc Dimittis* sprang from his heart as he beheld the infant in his arms. "Now let thy servant depart in peace"

(Luke 2:29). At last Simeon's soul felt emancipated in accordance with Isaiah's promise of so long ago (52:1).

Only God can emancipate the soul. True, in Buddhism an awakened ego that surrenders itself to the Buddha essence and transcends the veils of illusion may also experience release from the cycles of a crippling ego. Surely, the Lotus Chambers of God's heart include all God's children who seek what their contrite natures implore?

Perhaps only an emancipated soul can experience the consolation that Simeon acknowledged as he beheld Mary's wondrous boy. He claimed it for his own: the unparalleled solace that the holiness of God bestows.

Dear God, help us to know that solace, too. Encourage us to set our troubled egos free! Help us to pass beyond the veils of illusion to rest our hearts in your pure love and perfect peace.

~~~

"The Spirit of the LORD is upon me, because he has anointed me to bring good news to the poor." (Luke 4:18)

Luke tells us that Jesus read the above text from the scroll that was handed him. The selection Jesus read is from Isaiah 61 in reference to Judah's longing for the Messiah. In Jesus' time, he had yet to come, though misguided pretenders appeared from time to time. In today's world, we are cautious of self-proclaimed messiahs. Only God can anoint his chosen one, or those whom God selects to anoint others. Samuel anointed Saul; later he anointed David; Zadok and Nathan anointed Solomon; Elisha anointed Jehu; Jehoiada anointed Joash. YWHW considered Cyrus his "anointed one." Not all God's anointed turned out to be wholesome or perfect. Still, they were God's anointed. Their task was to bring good news to the poor. Their very presence symbolized the possibility of redressing age-old sorrows and anguished grievances. God's anointed were under God's commission to actualize his will for justice and righteousness, for goodness and fairness, and for the necessary measure of life's sustaining "milk and honey." It required the "Spirit of the LORD" indwelling a Messiah for God's anointed to address and fulfill his promises. That Saul, Jehu, and Joash faltered along the way should not discourage us. None of God's anointed was perfect. Even David and Solomon had their faults. That we too should stumble is understandable. Not a whit of this diminishes God's gracious kindness and hope for humankind. That he can use even the fallen, even us, to his glory is the point.

Like Jesus, we too have been handed the holy scrolls of God's longing for all humankind. To bring good news to the poor does not require anointment. Not even ordination. Nonetheless, mankind yearns for God's good news and the comfort it brings. Indeed, whenever we venture in the name of the LORD to offer his hope and consolation, hearts are lifted and souls nurtured again.

In ancient India, to behold a *sadhu*, or holy man, was to receive *darshan*, a "blessing." In countless villages, it is still the case. Where Buddhism prevails, to fill a monk's bowl with rice carries the same blessing. Mankind hungers for God's good news, for God's messengers of promise whose words elevate the spirit, or whose very presence symbolizes God's immanence.

Years ago, I was a young pastor in the mountains of rural Virginia. I can still hear the joyous cries of the children who ran down the clay paths from their houses to greet me. They would shout: "Mama, Mama, it's the preacher!" I was their conduit of *darshan*. Their happy faces and bright eyes filled my own beggar's bowl with humility and tears. God needs us to be *darshan* for others, to lift their hearts with hope, just as Christ has lifted ours.

∿∿∿

"He has sent me to proclaim release to the captives and recovery of sight to the blind." (Luke 4:18)

Are we not all "captives," in some measure, of debilitating desires and blind inclinations, of past and present sorrows and dashed dreams? Who among us cannot recount his or her mistakes, disappointments, and disillusionments, or moments of jealousy, anger, envy, and spite? To be released from all that and its burden would be a rebirth, a *renovatio*. Jesus proclaims that it has already happened. That it is already available. Your release has already occurred. Perhaps that is why Luke adds "and recovery of sight to the blind"; inasmuch as we are too blind to realize, too codependent upon our own depression, to claim the peace that God has already made possible.

The depression of the heart can be very appealing. So long as we are depressed, or cast down, or know ourselves to be victims of endless disappointments—even of noble efforts—we have an excuse for not having to engage in the positive practice of kindness and goodwill. The wounded heart wants all these for itself, to compensate for its sorrows and unfulfilled dreams. Yet, they are the very means of healing that make our own redemption viable.

To forgive another, to seek out another, to listen to another frees the other person's "captive" heart and encourages self-healing and forgiveness. Indeed, it is the way of redemption, both for others and ourselves.

~~~

They were astounded at his teaching, for he taught them as one having authority. (Mark 1:22)

Perhaps there can be no true consolation without a foundation to support it. Otherwise, we are awash once again in our delusions and broken dreams; in our inability to climb out of our wells of disappointment. They were "astounded," literally, or in Greek: "struck out of one's wits," "amazed" (*ekplésso*).

Today we struggle with a plethora of astonishments, but so few bring us peace. On the contrary, one by one each brings us down a little lower, amazed, if not shocked by the violence and greed that nibble at the cords of existence.

There's a parable in the religious traditions of Jainism that tells of a man chased by a tiger into a pit. Clinging desperately to a hemp rope, he stares down into the black well beneath him. To his horror, it writhes with vipers. As he glances up again, he beholds a pair of mice, nibbling hungrily on the hemp. Suddenly, an elephant charges out of the jungle and butts a tree, overhanging the well. To his *astonishment*, honey begins to drip from a comb in its trunk, providing him with relief from his thirst. But, in revenge, oh, how the bees surround his lips and sting his chapped mouth! So, on he clings, suspended in a hopeless hope, realizing the brevity of his mortal nature, his loneliest loneliness.

Jainism came to India in a time of great despair, societal dysfunction, poverty, and utter hopelessness. Jainism became India's stoicism, a call for realism, personal sacrifice, courage, and endurance. Its parables were not meant to mock its people, but to jolt them into bucking up and taking charge of their lives.

Jesus was not a Jain. The founder of Jainism was a contemporary of the Buddha's. Each sought to console their nation's poor, discouraged, and elite alike with a message of encouragement. What Jesus offers is different, though a form of the same. Jesus' message can awaken us, too, if we'll but let it. "The kingdom of God is at hand. Repent and believe in the good news." That is our consolation, our jolt out of our wits. God is alive; God is present; his kingdom is at hand! Come! Accept his presence. Accept God's will. God's love! And all that is unclean, unclear, and uncertain will become clean, clear, and certain again.

~~~

He came and took her by the hand and lifted her up. (Mark 1:31b)

She was Simon Peter's mother-in-law. He was in Peter's home as a guest. She was ill, in fever. He came to her side, took her hand in his, and lifted her up. Strangely, how quickly her fever left! Quietly, she hurried to the kitchen to let him know how much she appreciated what he had done and, doing what custom had taught her to do from time immemorial, "she served them," Mark adds.

Have we ever asked ourselves, "Is he at my door, today? Come to my house to take my hand in his? To lift me to my feet, while his fingers absorb the fever of my being in the palm of his holy hand?"

She ran to serve him, to thank him. "Precious God! That you should come to my own house today, and offer me your hand, and I should not take it! O Beloved of Galilee! O Fairest of all! Take my hand now! My whole life with it! My fever! My rising up and lying down! My hopes and fears! My dreams and wildest aspirations!

That I too might rise again, climb off my bed of disappointment and sorrow, in order to serve You, yes, You, and my fellow man!"

∽∽∽

But he answered, "It is written, 'One does not live by bread alone …'"
(Matt 4:4a)

It was Jesus' response to the Tempter. That Tempter of old, who fain would placate our worst fears! He comes to us in the wilderness of our self-decay, our anger, our longing for self-fulfillment, and revenge. He stirs our gnawing restlessness to exacerbate that bottomless pit of disquietude within. He is today's dark angel of our better nature that God so wonderfully created. "Did God really say?" He sows his seeds of doubt in our souls. "There is no consolation save in what I prescribe," he states without blinking.

Jesus knew otherwise. He would not be enticed to change stones into bread. There is a hunger that far exceeds the cry of existence. Yes, the truly starving cannot live without bread. But once that hunger has been satisfied, there are deeper passions that vie for satiation. With what manna shall we feed them? With the stale loaves of discontentment and enmity? Paul makes a searing list of them: factions, envy, idolatry, strife—along with a multitude of self-annihilating lusts, from those of the eye to the lips to the flesh.

In contrast, Paul counterbalances them with his unique scale of positive opposites: love, joy, peace, patience, kindness, generosity, faithfulness, gentleness, and self-control. They alone console the heart. To paraphrase St. Augustine and Aristotle, it is in doing good that we become good, in being just that we become just, in loving that we receive love, and in acting courageously that we become courageous. We cannot become patient without being patient, or kind without being kind. It is in giving that we receive, in being faithful and merciful that we ourselves are blessed, and in forgiving that we are forgiven. To be gentle, tender, joyful, and of comfort to others enriches our own consolation. Finally, is it not in self-control—Paul's last virtue—that we surmount the darker angels of our nature?

The devil tempted Jesus twice again, failed, then sulked away in search of us.

~~~

"In the world you have tribulation; but be of good cheer, I have overcome the world." (John 16:33)

How comforting Jesus' words, just when we want to despair. We hate to give up our despair, because it affords numerous occasions for secondary gain. Nonetheless, the latter's compensatory value eventually fades. You can only endure self-pity so long before having to pick up the pieces of your life and move on. Dejection, depression, and low self-esteem are debilitating disorders of our time. They have always been facets of the world's tribulation, as Jesus diagnosed it. At one time or other we have all been tempted to withdraw into our loneliest loneliness, and there, hanging our harps on Babylon's willows, cease to believe in God's order of goodness and hope. Consequently, we fall into what Sartre once called "a gloomy quietism." But God's order of goodness is real, if we have the eyes to see and the will to believe. "Be of good cheer! I have overcome the world."

Tribulation is part of our lives, part of the world's tapestry. Contrary to what many may think, Jesus was not an idealist whose spiritual and personal program summoned people to abandon the world. Nor did he found a cult whose sole purpose was to escape the rigors of life.

During the mid-twentieth century, the philosopher Sartre proclaimed that words like "anguish, forlornness [and] despair" define the human condition. For Sartre, faith in God was not an option. One had to assume the "anguish" of becoming responsible for oneself, if not for others in a brotherhood without God. In turn, this led to "forlornness," in as much as without God there can be no absolute Value or universal Good. One has to create and justify one's own. All of which led to his definition of "despair"— meaning that mankind had to confine itself to "reckoning only with what depends on our will," as life's "ensemble of probabilities" affects us.

Sartre acknowledged that such an agenda called for an "optimistic toughness," which only a few would attain, in his judgment.[2]

Over against Sartre's analysis stands Jesus' own "optimistic toughness." It was one he lived, proclaimed, and admonished: "Seek ye first the kingdom of God and his righteousness and matters of shelter, raiment, and nourishment will fall into place." In no way was Jesus dismissing the forlornness that accompanies the political, economic, and social aspects of the human condition. What he offers amid the world's "ensemble of probabilities" is the kingdom of God with its universal and far-reaching rule: "Do unto others as you would have them do unto you." Yes, we are obligated to pursue the fairest systems of justice we can create, but Jesus' call to love and kindness, mercy and trust in God, eradicates all need for secondary gain.

~·~·~

"Blessed are you that weep now, for you shall laugh." (Luke 6:21b)

Jesus did not want our weeping to have the final word. Nor did the author of Ecclesiastes. "There is a time to weep and a time to laugh" (Eccl 3:4). Sometimes our hardest weeping occurs after days of laughter and happiness, of sunshine and joy. It was so with Job as well as David, weeping over the death of Bathsheba's first-born and later the death of his son, Absalom. "O Absalom! Absalom!" In the wisdom tradition, there is a time for both tears and laughter, as well as sorrow and joy.

In Luke's Gospel, those who *weep* are clearly the poor, the disabled, and disenfranchised. They symbolize the bereft of every nation and every culture. Theirs is the weeping of the hungry, the downtrodden, the discounted, and dispossessed. Unfortunately, they slip through every safety net. Their numbers have been monitored since the time of Caesar Augustus' census of Palestine, indeed, as far back as the time of Solomon, if not the time of the pharaohs and the kings of Akkad and Sumer. They crowded around Jesus and

2. See Jean Paul Sartre's *Existentialism*, trans. Bernard Frechtman (New York: Philosophical Library, 1947).

found hope in his presence, his voice, his tender message and loving mercy. "Blessed are you who weep," said Jesus, "who have wept, still weep, and long for the day of deliverance. It will come. In fact, it has come and is waiting for you to grasp." Indeed, however much each might have wept, Mark tells us that "the great throng heard him gladly" (Mark 12:37).

∼∼∼

"Daughters of Jerusalem, do not weep for me,
but weep for yourselves." (Luke 23:28)

There is a level of weeping as devastating as hunger, if not more so. It is the weeping of the soul. Contrite and broken, it rises from the heart and waits in silence for the advent of the Messiah, for the long-awaited passing of Jesus' shadow. It is the weeping of the deep calling to the Deep. "Out of the depths I cry to thee, O LORD! . . . If thou shouldst mark iniquities, who could stand?" (Ps 130:1, 3). Paul made the same cry: "O wretched man that I am! Who will deliver me from this body of death?" (Rom 7:24). It is the universal lament of the wretched, the lapsed, and the fallen—the lament of the wise even more so. One cannot go on limping between the Eternal and the Baals of culture, between the altar of YWHW and the altars of emptiness, without one's heart breaking into.

> A voice is heard in Ramah,
> Wailing and loud lamentation,
> Rachel is weeping for her children,
> And refuses to be comforted . . . (Jer 31:15)

The poet Rilke expressed it just as masterfully:

> Whoever just now weeps anywhere in the world,
> Without cause weeps in the world,
> Weeps over me.[3]

---

3. Rainer Maria Rilke, *Selected Poems*, trans. C. F. MacIntyre (Berkeley: University of California Press, 1940). The above verses of "Solemn Hour" are the author's own translation.

Rilke understood the brokenness of the human condition that cannot find its way back to wholeness, purity, or peace. Jesus understood it too, and offered the way back.

"Peace I leave with you," said Jesus. "My peace I give unto you. . . . Let not your hearts be troubled, neither let them be afraid" (John 14:27).

~~~

*He saw a great throng, and he had compassion on them, because they were like sheep without a shepherd. (Mark 6:34)*

As a child on a farm, I often marveled at the sheep. It was on my grandmother's farm. We had no shepherd, nor a sheep dog. They were on their own. A few wore bells, so we could know where they were at night or in bad weather. Their shelter consisted of a long shed, provided with feed troughs and straw under a roof of rusted tin, supported by poles taken from the forest of the "Knobs," as we called them. A nearby creek served as their watering hole. Men came from neighboring farms to help shear them in the spring. Huge piles of dirty wool were loaded onto wagons and driven into town for sale. No one really worried about the sheep except in winter. That's when the ewes gave birth to their lambs, in the heart of cold winter, when the ground lay frozen and glistening with frost, or covered with snow. Then the dogs came, one or two at first, then in packs. Like their cousins, the wolves, they'd steal in at night and chase the sheep, scattering ewes and lambs alike, killing them strictly for the sport. It broke my heart when my uncles and brother fanned out across the hills at night with guns to eliminate the dogs. I can still see one canine's eyes, glowing in the frost of that cold night, before the gun's report echoed up the long hill. When the ewes went down, their orphaned lambs had to be fed. Then my heart would fill with joy, as I nursed the little lambs with warm milk from a heated Pepsi bottle with a nipple on it as large as a lemon. Now the sheep are gone, but the farm's still there, where deer come down at night to graze where sheep once fed.

O shepherd of Bethlehem, how your sheep need you today as much as they did of old!

~~~

And he awoke and rebuked the wind, and said to the sea, "Peace! Be
still!" And . . . there was a great calm. (Mark 4:39)

The stilling of the storm has more to do with the gales that buf-
fet our hearts than with the winds that endangered the little fleets
of Galilee. It is our tiny craft, our infinitesimal life, set against the
infinity of the universal Sea that calls our life into question. Why
are we afraid, so fearful of each wave, as if we weren't given hearts
large enough to believe and trust in God's goodness? Why do we
have such little faith, whether in ourselves or others? As for the disciples, why did they have to awaken their Master, when he was in
their midst all along? Indeed, was he not literally "in the same boat"
with them? O, ye of little faith! And so he calmed the sea, rebuked
the wind, and shamed the waves with his Father's voice from deep
within.

Amid the chaos and crises of life, God is as close to us as our
slightest whisper. His is still "the still small voice"—that essence of
calm and equanimity that results in the highest peace. This in no
way diminishes the terror we feel when life's seas rise above us, or
their waves crash upon us, leaving us awash in violent riptides that
drag us back into the Deep. Life's winds and waves and crashing
seas are part of creation's mystery. The vortex that keeps the oceans
moving draws in new life, new air, new seas, and vast schools of
nutrients to balance the hemispheres cycles that energize the earth's
orbiting marvel. It cannot be otherwise. To wish it so would make
a mockery of God's universe, if not a mockery of God. Paul says it
so well:

> More than that, we rejoice in our sufferings,
> knowing that suffering produces endurance,
> and endurance produces character, and character
> produces hope, and hope does not disappoint us,
> because God's love has been poured out into our hearts
> through the Holy Spirit, which has been given to us.
> (Rom 5:3–5)

We do not have to settle for minimal faith. As difficult as it is to rise above adversity, the Son of Galilee's words call us to trust his presence. They summons us to belief anew in his Father's ordering of the universe. He calls us to greater faith in spite of the winds and waves that threaten our storm-tossed crafts, or fill us with panic and the temptation to disbelieve. We do not have to waver. We do not have to awaken the Savior in our hearts. Can we not let him rest, or his humanity within us even sleep? Can we not man the craft, or trim its sails, or steady its rudder long enough for the Savior to renew his own strength within us for those hours when we shall need him most? What a privilege to watch over and with the Savior in our hearts, to stand with him and for him amid life's ineffable storms and fierce seas! To be his mate, his truest mate, like a saintly Odysseus, faithful and fearless to the end!

≈≈≈

"[My] peace I give unto you; not as the world giveth,
give I unto you." (John 14:72 KJV)

The year was 1986. The place: Debrecen, Hungary. The occasion: the IV International Congress for Calvin Research. Attendees: scholars from across the Continent, the United Kingdom (Scotland and Britain), North America, South Africa, the Soviet Bloc, Asia, Japan, Korea. We flew into Budapest from our respective countries and were driven by bus across the great plains of Hungary to Debrecen. The harvest lay all about us: mounds of squash, melons, cabbage, and produce—all of it the labor of collective farms, still under the management of the Soviet system. No one was in sight in the fields. Our hosts stopped for us to enjoy a break in the midst of Hungary's vast, fertile steppes. There, in the crowded lounge of a village's central store, sat a dozen or more men, drinking beer and watching a Clint Eastwood movie on TV. They perked up when they heard our voices and smiled when we greeted them, some of us in English, most in German. We drove on to Debrecen to engage in a week of spirited papers and addresses on Calvin, presented by different members, mainly from Canada, Scotland, France, Switzerland, West Germany, and East Germany. Members of the

Communist Party attended the opening session and monitored our speeches and singing of Reformed and Hungarian hymns. The air was electric with excitement. One could have been in Geneva, or Basel, or Wittenberg, when the Hapsburgs were in power and faith came at the risk of one's life.

But it was not so. The scholars reached across the barriers of time and language, distance and culture, to immerse in the grace of God as the Reformed tradition has championed Calvin's views across the years. After the conference concluded, a Hungarian professor invited us to his home in northeastern Hungary. Our tiny caravan of cars and buses wended its way into the low mountains of Transylvania and into the heartland of old Bohemia. Along the way, we passed a town in which the ruins of a Jewish synagogue, burned during the Nazi era, rose in blackened sorrow to stare at us through its ancient sanctuary's rafters. The black holes of its once magnificent windows haunted us as we passed its lonely hulk, still standing since its *Kristallnacht* of horror some fifty years earlier. *Alors!* How we drew back in shock, even shame! That this could have happened in our time! Later that evening, after dinner, our host invited us into his *cave*, or wine cellar, where we tasted the fruit of his vines from the many casks that enwalled the cellar. Then the wife of an attending scholar from East Germany, calling to mind the abomination of desolations we had witnessed earlier, led us in singing "*Dona Nobis Pacem.*" She divided us into three groups, mine consisting of a Canadian, two Hungarians, a scholar from Japan, John H. Leith,[4] and myself. The two other groups were comprised of French, Scots, Brits, Germans, and South Africans. Our voices rose in hope and harmony, yet longing and sorrow, knowing that peace comes only at great cost, effort, love, faith in God, and the determination that no Holocaust must ever recur.

4. Former professor of historical theology at Union Theological Seminary.

# 3

# Jesus as Healer

And Jesus went about all the cities and villages, teaching in their synagogues and preaching the gospel of the kingdom, and healing every disease and every infirmity. (Matt 9:35)

THE GREEK WORD FOR healing is *therapeuon*, from whence we derive our own word "therapy." How more contemporary could Matthew's text be? He provides a picture of Jesus in his larger role as a compassionate practitioner, whose therapeutic program is adjunct to his teaching and evangelical activity. All this he practices in synagogues and public squares alike. Indeed, is it not this same living Jesus who comes to us today as he came to those of old? Is it not he who extends his hand to heal us and cast out our demons, whatever the form of therapy he deems best? Are we willing for him to cleanse us, to cast out our demons and unclean spirits?

Jesus' exorcisms, healings, and compassionate words are as needed now as then. To have our own fevers calmed, our brokenness mended, and sorrows, disorders, and illnesses healed by his touch, by his spiritual presence and patient heart, would be a boon indeed. "Behold, I stand at the door and knock; if any one hears my voice and opens the door, I will come in . . ." (Rev 3:20).

~~~

> Just then there was in their synagogue a man with an unclean spirit,
> and he cried out, "What have you to do with us, Jesus of Nazareth?
> Have you come to destroy us? I know who you are, the Holy One
> of God." But Jesus rebuked him, saying, "Be silent, and come out
> of him!" And the unclean spirit, convulsing him and crying
> with a loud voice, came out of him. (Mark 1:23–26)

Biblical commentaries and dictionaries focus numerous articles on the Old Testament's absorption with "clean" and "unclean." The ancient world rightly wrestled with contagious diseases that had the potential of spreading through the Fertile Crescent's nomadic and urban populations. Skin eruptions, dermatological anomalies, and loss of blood called for immediate attention, often falling under a priest's scrutiny. The books of Leviticus and Numbers describe and prescribe the priest's duty. Great steps were taken to restore cleanness before the prognosis of "unclean" was declared. But once declared *unclean*, the unclean were often expelled to live in colonies and communities of their own,

Clean and unclean, however, carry other connotations as well, especially in our world today. Thanks to Freud and Jung, we know that we all carry a level of repressed disorder in our subconsciousness. The Psalmist recognized as much, too, attributing it to "sin": "For I know my transgressions, and my sin is ever before me" (Ps 51:3). In that line composed by David, his grief plummeted with the reality that even from birth his inclination was toward rebellion and suppressed desires—"I was brought forth in iniquity, and in sin did my mother conceive me" (51:5). How do we rid ourselves of such innate generic inclinations to resist what is good and to question what is holy? Such a dark side shadows our waking humanity as well as haunts our dreams. There, in the slumber of our subconscious, our unconscious self wrestles with indomitable nightmares, unresolved forebodings, and fragile longings. Who has not dreamed of fleeing from wolves only too succumb as the pack closes in and, then awaken feverish, numb, and all too aware that something isn't right?

Note that the man's cry for help occurs in the synagogue, his people's holy place for prayer and study. He knew where to flee, where to seek solace. He knew what he needed, whom he needed: "I know who you are, the Holy One of God." And he knew why Jesus was there: "Have you come to destroy us?" Now, all his demons, all his misgivings and repressions unite to safeguard his disintegrated self. Jesus had to "rebuke" him. "Listen! Be not deceived. It is you I have come to redeem. Come out, now, and be whole!" And it was only with "convulsions" and "crying with a loud voice" that all that had kept him unclean came out, and then only because of the Master's voice, the Master's love, and the Master's power of God within.

Precious God, we too need that cleansing. Even your loving rebuke! We too know why you have come. We too know who you are. O Holy One of God! O Blessed Son of Mary.

~~~

And behold a leper came to him and knelt before him, saying,
"LORD, if you will, you can make me clean."
And he stretched out his hand and touched him, saying,
"I will; be clean." . . . and his leprosy was cleansed. (Matt 8:2–3)

Leprosy today is known as "Hansen's Disease." Gone is the leper colony of Moloka'i, Hawaii, founded in 1865 to protect Hawaii's vulnerable population. The colony treated lepers from its very founding, and then under Father Damien and his order of Catholic sisters, and later under others until 1969. So also the leper colony of Carville, Louisiana, would witness its own rise and demise, though treatment for the bacterial infection is still available. The shocking scenes of Lou Wallace's leprosy pits in *Ben Hur* may have been exaggerated, but the physical, spiritual, and mental suffering it caused its sufferers is no travesty of woe. Sufferers of psoriasis and other skin infections know only too well the discomfort and embarrassment of having to hide their patches of scaly and itchy skin from gawkers' views. In that sense, they are no different than Wallace's lepers, bound in their infectious rags.

Jesus *touched* the leper in Matthew's story. He reached out and touched his scaly flesh with his Father's fingertips and answered the man's cry from the depth of his own heart: "I will; be clean."

Does not Jesus reach out to us in the same way today? "I will; be clean." He never questioned the man, did he? He never probed into his past, or asked for a resumé, or demanded a litany of changes he expected the leper to promise. "Go show yourself to the priest, to those whom Moses authorized to pronounce you clean." Whether he went or not, or a priest pronounced him clean, nonetheless, he was clean in Jesus' eyes, both in body and spirit.

It can happen to us—to be clean in spirit and heart again; to stand with others in the holy places of prayer and teaching, cleansed in conscience and soul, set at liberty from the leper's colony of our shame-hidden lives.

~~~

"LORD, my servant is lying paralyzed at home, in terrible distress."
(Matt 8:6)

When I was a young minister, I often visited the home of a paralyzed man who, as a painter, had fallen from a ladder, never to walk again. He was a quadriplegic, and his wife had to assist him in everything. Sometimes I would steady his shoulders, while his wife brought him something to drink, or wiped his lips, or tears from his eyes. I would place my hand on his arm, though I knew he couldn't feel it, but his eyes always filled with gratitude. His wife would sit with us, for her own comfort as much as his. She needed our visits, too. She held his hands and found as much strength in the Psalms and in the New Testament passages I read as did he. Both were humble, so grateful for my visits. Time and again I would leave with tears in my own eyes, wondering if I had read the right words, the most helpful passages, or had prayed as comforting a prayer as I might have.

How I wanted Jesus to be there! For the Savior to touch the bed-ridden man and heal him of his "terrible distress"! It was not so. But God was there, nonetheless. You could sense his presence in the bright sunlit room that the man's wife kept to perfection; in the loving and patient manner she cared for him and greeted me, as well as in the way she fluffed his pillow and combed back his hair; and above all in the simple tidiness of the clean and fragrant room, arranged with flowers and photos of their children on the windowsills for her husband to see. And he was there in the quadriplegic's eyes; in the suffering he bore in silence; in his calm confinement and repose; and in the patience with which he bore his paralysis.

Sometimes we see God only in the suffering of others, in the hurt and loneliness that tragedy has brought their way. God is there, in all of that, along with the strength he gives to endure each day. He comes to us in his summons to visit the sick and the elderly, the poor and distressed, the lonely, the heartbroken, the homeless, and bereft. There he awaits our love and generous gifts. It is said that Rabbi Nahum of Stepinesht once commented to his Hasidic followers, "If we could hang all our sorrows on pegs and were allowed to choose those we liked best, every one of us would take back his own, for all the rest would seem even more difficult to bear."[1]

∼∼∼

Again he entered the synagogue, and a man was there
who had a withered hand ... (Mark 3:1)

We do not know the origin of the man's withered hand. Thousands suffered from physical abnormalities, birth defects, and withered feet, hands, and limbs. They were as prevalent in Jesus' day as in our own. We know them to be traceable to genetic anomalies. In his era, the deformations were thought to be the result of parental or personal sin, as if God deliberately punished the innocent for the sins of the fathers. It was a hard conviction to dispel. Modern medicine and the miracle of plastic surgery constitute today's anodyne for one's restoration to health and healing. "Who will ever want to kiss me?" a young girl asked her craniofacial specialist, as he examined her distorted lips. "We will do all that we can," he replied. But as he told the story to me, lines of memory still etched themselves deeply

---

1. Martin Buber, *Tales of the Hasidim*, trans. Olga Marx (New York: Schochen, 1971), 2:73.

about the corners of his mouth. "We did our best," he added. "Actually, we did quite good, but a scar was still there."

Mark explains that the healing of the man with the withered hand occurred on a Sabbath, in a synagogue, where once again the wounded knew where to go. So also Jesus' critics had gathered about, watching to see what Jesus would do. They never let up; they never relaxed, just as they never relax today.

They put Jesus to the question with their eyes, with their judgmental glances and looks. How they broke his heart and tempted his spirit, but he bore them with the magnanimity of God. "Is it lawful to do good or to do harm on the Sabbath, to save life or to kill?" They ground their teeth in silence. "Stretch out your hand," said Jesus, and in that instant, the man's withered hand was restored.

We may or may not have a withered hand, a withered arm, a craniofacial disfigurement, but Jesus' words can still *restore* our withered lives. What is more, following his example, we can care for the *withered* too. For it is better to do the best we can than to render harm or cause others to despair. Right now I wager there is a silent sufferer waiting for your phone call or mine, or visit at this very hour.

∾∾∾

That evening they brought to him many who were possessed
with demons; and he cast out the spirits with a word . . . (Matt 8:16)

We do not call them demons today, but their behavior and consequential fallout well assume demonic proportions. Check out any list of disorders, and you will find them catalogued and explained: from dysthymia (self-doubt) to depression, bipolar to borderline, obsessive-compulsive to panic, post-traumatic to social phobias, down to common anxiety and schizophrenia—all potentially demonic—not to mention alcoholism, or drug and sex addictions. Nor have we even mentioned disillusionment, anger, enmity, spite, greed, or jealousy. All are demonic, and each of us, in his or her own way, has been possessed or victimized by their presence. Can they be cast out? Matthew says, "Yes!" Jesus did it with a single word: "Out!"

Today's physicians prescribe single words too: Prozac, Lexapro, Zoloft, Wellbutrin, and others. This is not said to make light of life's demons, or of any of life's healing medications from God, or from his creation. Nonetheless, there are other words that bring healing too, sacred anodynes for casting out demons. We know them as love, kindness, faith, hope, patience, gentleness, charity, courage, and self-control. Yes, they are difficult to practice, to inculcate into our lives. Which is why we need Jesus, beside us, before us, behind us, within us, casting out our demons with his own word of love. We need his presence and power within, his word and strength overpowering our weakness and fears. "LORD, here am I, demons and all! Cast me not away from your presence. Fill me with your goodness and kindness that my words might be healing, too, and my hands and heart an extension of your own."

~·~·~

Now he was casting out a demon that was dumb; when the demon had gone out, the dumb man spoke, and the people marveled. (Luke 11:14)

She had been in the hospital two weeks. They had placed her in the psychiatric ward. Her minister asked me to visit her. He had driven in to see her thrice, but he couldn't get her to respond to a single word. She had become catatonic, deeply withdrawn and numb. Her residence? Norfolk. Her diagnosis? Catatonia with severe depression. Why? How could it be? She was so young and beautiful and looked so healthy. She sat with her feet curled in her lap. A pink bathrobe covered her yellow nightgown. They had combed her hair, though they had taken away her wedding bands and earrings. Why was she here, in this hospital in particular, on the sixth floor overlooking the naval yard, on such a sunny day? "You know why she's there?" her minister told me. "Out of loneliness, out of brokenness. Her husband's ship's tied up in berth right there for all to see. But where is he? On board! Why? Because whenever his ship puts in, he volunteers to remain aboard to impress the admiral. Think of it! Without a thought of her! It's happened over and over again with countless navy wives. Maybe you can get her to speak, to cry, just anything to dredge her back from despair."

45

So I went. I was younger then; healthy, frightened and curious, all in the same breath. I sat opposite her. I felt so awkward. What was I to do? To say? To read? Or was I just to sit there in silence with her? I studied her eyes, her mouth, her hands. "You know why I've come," I offered. "My father was in the service too. When he went off to the Aleutians in '41, I was just a boy of six. I didn't see him for another three years. I know you must be lonely. X told me why you're here. My heart breaks for you." Maybe tears welled up. I don't remember. I smiled. She smiled too. She reached for my hand. I reached for hers. "May I offer a prayer?" I asked. She shook her head, yes. "Dear God, please be with your lonely daughter and love her into wholeness again." Some things you never forget. Nor have I forgotten her, sitting there in her gown, waiting to be filled with the Word of Life again.

~·~·~

"If I touch even his garments, I shall be made well."
And immediately the hemorrhage ceased. (Mark 5:28–29)

"She had suffered much," writes Mark, "under many physicians, and had spent all that she had, and was no better but rather grew worse." I remember a parishioner who suffered back pain for years. Weekly, she sought relief from a trusted therapist who treated her with massages and hot towels. Occasionally, she found relief from prescribed muscle relaxants. No one ever thought that her condition might be exacerbated by cancer. Gradually, her health deteriorated and her pain increased. When finally she could bear it no longer, she changed physicians to discover the truth about her back and the origin of her pain. She died less than two months later. How much money she spent, only her husband knew. That she suffered, everyone could see. How she must have longed to touch if only the hem of the Master's garment!

Mark explains that a profound factor of many of Jesus' healings is the role a sufferer's faith played in his or her recovery. Faith cannot always eradicate the ravages of disease nor reverse a terminal illness. But faith can restore one's hope, renew one's love of family and neighbor, and bestow inner peace, day by day. The stages of death and dying apply to illnesses as well. The journey from denial to bargaining, from postponement to acceptance, is a journey we have all experienced, a road we have often traveled. The woman in Mark's text was on that journey too. "If only I can touch!" Perhaps it is only after we have spent fortunes uselessly to allay our disappointments and sufferings that it finally occurs to us to reach out to that one source of wholeness who is always there: the Savior as he passes by. Her faith enabled Jesus to fill her soul and body with his wholeness and balm, which only he can bestow. Like an electrical shock, he felt his Father's power pass into her, cleansing and restoring her to health again.

That identical faith is available to us, if we will but reach for the hem of his love. "Save me, O LORD, for my life is seeping away. Have not I, too, wasted so many resources that You have so kindly given me?" God in Christ heard her whispered prayer; surely he awaits and hears ours too!

≈≈≈

Now there is in Jerusalem . . . a pool, . . . which has five porticoes. In these lay a multitude of invalids, blind, lame, paralyzed. One man was there, who had been ill for thirty-eight years. When Jesus saw him . . . he said, "Do you want to be healed?" (John 5:2–6)

If ever a man had been his own passive-aggressive victim, it was this unknown pliant beside the Bethzatha pool. Legend had it that, from time to time, an angel descended from heaven to stir the waters of the pool, and that whosoever managed first to make it into the spring would be healed. A cruel jest, one might argue, even for God to deign. But that isn't John's point in telling the story. It was a Sabbath, and once again Jesus' critics were watching. Why was this invalid carrying his pallet on the Sabbath? He knew the Sabbath rules. Who did he think he was? And by whose authority had he dared to violate the tradition of the fathers? More than illness was at stake, more even than God's presence and power to heal. "My Father is working still, and I am working too."

We could demythologize this story, as contemporary scholars of more recent New Testament versions have done. One can simply delete the legend of the descending angel and remove the mystery and longing of God's muffled rustling in life's sacred springs. Or one could replace the angel with dogmatic principles rather than with the awe and wonder of God's descent into our troubled midst. It's a wonder the scholars haven't removed Luke's multitude of heavenly hosts singing in the highest, or his babe in a manger, or the gawking shepherds, or weary wise men traveling from the East, following yonder star. Isn't it all the same principle? The same saga and journey of mankind's longing for God? What purpose is achieved in deleting the descending angel? Should we cast ballots to remove Jacob's angel as well, or David's slingshot, or Moses' upraised arms that held back the raging waves of the Red Sea? O these "mice of the scrolls," as Ezra Pound was fond of labeling them!

Still, the truth is there in John's story. It cannot be swept aside as a gloss. For in truth, sometimes *we don't want* to be healed. It's so much safer to cling to our multitude of dysfunctions and maladaptive practices. To what Adler called "attention, power, revenge, and inadequacy." We know how to function that way, to manipulate ourselves and others. "I have no one to help me, to carry me to the pool, LORD. Please don't ask or expect me to do more!" But the descending Christ will not be so easily deterred, as if he were only a gloss on the margin of the Gospel. No. You have to want to be healed. You have to want to be changed. To realize that alone on your pallet you will forever be weak and vulnerable. "Do you want to be healed?" He asks us. Can't you hear it in his voice? "Don't you want to be healed? Don't you want to be raised to life again by my Father's angels? How many more must he send before you dust off your pallet, yes, even crawl if you must, and stand on your feet, and help the nearest sufferer beside you to race toward that spring together? Remember, the first are always last. And in God's sight, the last are as prized as the first." And so Jesus healed him. The man stood erect, for the first time in thirty-eight years. He didn't even know Jesus' name. All he knew was that he was healed, just as you and I can be healed today. "Come," says Jesus. "This is a good day to be healed! Come. Let me take your hand."

∾∾∾

"And when you hear of wars and rumors of war …
this is but the beginning of the sufferings." (Mark 13:7–8)

One has to wonder if any veterans of Herod's wars lay among the paralyzed and blind in those porticoes of the Bethzatha pool. Simply maintaining order under the Romans alone would have taken its toll. The Gospels depict Jesus as a man of peace; still its writers mention kings and procurators, administrators, Herodians, princes, wars, soldiers, and even Caesar. So too are centurions, tribunes, legates, and proconsuls listed among its pages. Jesus would have passed numerous squads of Roman soldiers, as well as noted the Jewish guards assigned to protect the temple. Although Roman legions had their own surgeons and medical staffs, discharged soldiers and veterans of the temple guard might well have been among the maimed, paralyzed, and forgotten. Jesus went there, John tells us, perhaps at first to observe; then he set about his Father's business. "We must work the works of him who sent me, while it is day; night comes, when no one can work" (John 9:4).

As a teenager I was hospitalized with wounded soldiers returning from the Korean War. The time: 1951. The place: Percy Jones Army Hospital, Battle Creek, Michigan. My father, Lt. Col. Farley, was the hospital's director of medical supplies. The war still waged hot. Many of the veterans were recovering from horrid wounds, some having been there since World War II. Daily, Major Darby, the hospital's chief chaplain, made his rounds as best he could. Always good-natured, pleasant, and smiling, he directed his way from ward to ward, soldier to soldier. I was honored to be among them, recovering from a skiing injury. One day a visitor to our ward rattled some newspapers as she folded them to discard in a trash can. Everyone—lame, wounded, scarred, and burned—leapt from their beds to seek cover. I can still see their faces and hear their laughter afterwards. One man cried and had to be consoled. As I look back on it, I realize Christ was there. Yes, sometimes in the chaplain's visits, sometimes in the surgeon's dressing room, or in the daily programs and evening events sponsored by the USO and other organizations, but especially in the laughter and tears the wounded offered each other. They constituted their own portico, their own spring of restoration, where unseen angels descended from ward to ward to stir their hearts with hope and courage again.

We must not think lightly of Jesus' concern for the paralyzed, the lame, the blind, or wounded soldiers recovering from war's horror. Many of the latter were no doubt present at that portico and crowded about Jesus as he visited the spring.

∾∾∾

> "One thing I know, that though I was blind,
> now I see …" (John 9:25b)

Every Gospel reports at least one or more cases in which Jesus heals the blind. Blindness was common, as it still is in the Middle East. Various forms of ophthalmia, conjunctivitis, trachoma, glaucoma, and cataracts plagued the Judea of Jesus' day. Eye diseases were often transmitted by flies, aggravated by dust-driven winds, and intensified by the sun's glare. Jesus employed different therapeutic methods to cure the blind. He mixed the alkaline properties of salvia with clay, applying it gradually to the eyes, while directing his suppliants to wash their eyes in the cool waters of a neighboring pool.[2] Such is the case in John 9.

But it wasn't just optical blindness that the Gospel writers' wanted to highlight. It was the blindness of a generation's soul, the ophthalmia of a nation's heart and vision that needed to be probed. "I am the light of the world," Jesus said, though it angered the critics who watched the healing. Their hardness of heart weighed heavily on Jesus' own. Saddened by their disbelief, he consoled the healed man: "For judgment I came into this world, that those who do not see may see, and that those who see may become blind" (9:39). Suddenly, one of his critics realized the depth of his own default. "Are we also blind?" his conscience compelled him to ask. "That you must ask," replied Jesus, "answers your question."

2. See *The Interpreter's Dictionary of the Bible* (New York: Abingdon, 1962), 1:448–49. See also the author's *Jesus as Man, Myth, and Metaphor: Beyond the Jesus of History Debate* (Eugene, OR: Wipf and Stock, 2007), 149–151.

The truth is so plain to see, isn't it? How blind am I? Are you? What is it that I still cannot see, that dims my vision even now that constitutes that glaucoma of the spirit that won't be healed? LORD, heal my eyes, my vision, that I too may see more clearly, love more dearly, and serve more nearly as you would have me do.

∽∽∽

And they brought the boy to [Jesus]; and when the spirit saw him,
immediately it convulsed the boy, and he fell on the ground
and rolled about, foaming at the mouth. (Mark 9:20)

Anyone who has ever witnessed an epileptic seizure knows how terrifying those heartbreaking moments of the convulsions can be: the rolling of the eyes, the sickening features of the writhing face, the helplessness that sinks into everyone about, the sadness that immediately follows, and the embarrassed shame the epileptic feels.

The little girl in the barnyard picked herself up and stared at the rest of us. The event had silenced us all. I was standing on the steps of the granary. Dust still covered the little child's flour-sack dress, along with cracked grain and chicken feathers on her hands and little face. She looked at us: bewildered, in silence, as if a violent storm had passed through her, forever shattering the playful moment we had all enjoyed. Her little face still comes to me across the years, with her stringy hair, huge eyes, and bare feet, one rubbing the other as she teetered, numb and frightened. That was in the 1940s, when rural America had yet to climb its way out of backwardness and poverty, especially in the South.

Jesus moaned. "O faithless generation, how long am I to be with you? How long am I to bear with you? Bring the boy to me. How long as he had this?" he asked the father. "From childhood," the dispirited father replied. They talked some more. Then Jesus turned to the "unclean spirit" in the boy. "You dumb and deaf spirit, I command you, come out of him, and never enter again!" And after more writhing and tears, it came out, leaving "the boy like a corpse." But Jesus took him by the hand and lifted him up, and he became well.

There are medications we can take today, prescriptions for ourselves and our children—especially for our children. But there remain other forms of epilepsy that only Jesus' love can cast out; forms of bitterness, jealousy, rancor, revenge, and spite that only a broken and contrite heart can allow Jesus to begin to mend. Who has not witnessed friends or siblings so snarling at each other as to make ones heart cringe? Only love, repentance, and forgiveness can transform an evil heart. "Help my unbelief!" begged the father. And so Jesus healed the father's son, just as he can heal us, and would have healed the little girl, had he been present that day in that rural barnyard. Yet he was present! He was present in that little child's face, her eyes, her bewilderment, her silence, and in our frightened hearts too, as we witnessed her hollow stare and struggled with our own longing for God to help her, though we didn't know how to voice it as children. We just felt life's sting in our hearts.

≈≈≈

"Young man, I say to you, arise." And the dead man sat up,
and began to speak. (Luke 7:14–15)

The youth was the widow's only son, Luke tells us. Jesus watched the procession lament its way sadly through the streets. Luke tells us that when "the LORD saw her, he had compassion" and bade her not to weep. Then he placed his hands on the bier and commanded the young man to arise, and to everyone's amazement, the boy did. Two similar resuscitation stories are also preserved in the Gospels: the raising of Lazarus being the most famous, and Mark's story (5:21–24) the second.

The larger truth in this story shatters any surface complacency we might harbor. "Unless a grain of wheat falls into the earth and dies, it cannot bear fruit" (John 12:24). In countless respects, we are the widow's son or daughter. Moreover, there is an "only-ness" about our personhood that God has nurtured since the day we were conceived in our mother's womb (Ps 139:13).

Anyone who has ever read Tolstoy's *The Death of Ivan Ilych* may remember how his professional friends sought comfort in the thought: "It is he who is dead and not I." Perhaps Tolstoy had read Donne's line:

*Never send to know for whom the bell tolls, It tolls for thee.*

Spiritual death creeps into our souls in many forms. It carries an existential import, bordering on despair. Its origin can be the death of a loved one, the heartbreak of a relationship, the loss of a child; or it can spring from a failure that won't go away: economical, personal, or professional. It can also result from the exhaustion and deterioration of a disease, or from the onset of Alzheimer's in one's self, spouse, or parent, or from being victimized by an abusive friend or family member. All these result in the death of one's spirit, drowning one's will to live. Yet, perhaps that has to happen before we can be reborn, to be shocked out of our belief in the all-sufficiency of the self. "For whoever would save his life will lose it; and whoever loses his life for my sake and the gospels will save it" (Mark 8:35).

In the last moments of Ivan's life, Tolstoy describes the dying man's thoughts: that although he, Ivan, could not rectify his own life, he realized that love and forgiveness could and did. And he wanted so much to be able to say that to his wife and school-aged son. He *died in peace*, says Tolstoy, just as you and I can *live in peace*, if only we will stop clinging to our bier and let Christ fill us with life and joy again. Why? Because life is sacred, created by no one less than God, for us to enjoy as well as our neighbors.

≈≈≈

"One thing I know, that though I was blind,
now I see." (John 9:25)

So often our best insights come only after the damage has been done, or only after we've tumbled into the ditch. The story of Aaron Burr's duel with Alexander Hamilton is riveted in America's soul. The prolonged charges and animosity between the two had poisoned both leaders' senses. Their capacity for insult to their honor had reached its breaking point. Though outlawed in New York, the old *Code Duello* appealed to each as one's best way out. One could fire in the air to signal satisfaction, or take actual aim. Hamilton appears to have fired in the air, but his bullet struck a tree above Burr. The latter leveled his pistol, steadied his aim, and fired. Later Burr would quip that one ought never act precipitously, "because something may occur to make you regret your premature action." Still later he qualified his statement more: "Had I read Sterne [a novelist and Anglican clergyman] more and Voltaire less, I should have known the world was wide enough for both Hamilton and me."

Blindness of heart constitutes a spiritually crippling disorder. There arrived at Villemétie that summer a man in his thirties who had spent his past fifteen years in Chad and the French Cameroon, pedaling goods and services across those ancient sands. Exhausted and recuperating from an unknown disease, he embraced the life of the *équipe* with enthusiasm and joy. When asked if he didn't miss his adventuresome career, he explained only that his family and friends had encouraged him to come to André's Center that he might find a new direction for his life. As the year progressed, he never flinched from whatever duties André assigned him, nor did he ever question or doubt André's advice. As he confided once to me, he had come too close to that point of no return in Africa's deserts not to know that his wanderlust years had to cease. He had to come home if the next phase of his life were to be worth living.

How often have we not come to the point of no return, to look back across time and regret the precipitous actions we wish we hadn't taken? For Burr it was too late. For the wanderlust brother from Chad, it could not have occurred at a more opportune time. We cannot undo our past nor reverse its consequences. As a friend once said, "Once you ring the bell, you can't unring it." But at the feet of Christ, we can kneel and ask our LORD to heal our blindness of heart, our blindness of spirit, animosity, indifference, neglect, or unkindness; and, looking anew into his radiant face, see more clearly and act more lovingly, as he would have us do.

O Sacred LORD and Holy One, please hear our individual prayers. For we too have been blind in countless ways and squandered precious time in the sands of regret and the wilderness of our own undoing. Now, as we look back, we see how grace-filled a life can be that is hidden in Thee. Heal our blindness, O Son of God, that we too may see and love and be all that your heart longs for us to become.

# 4

# Jesus as Counselor-Companion

"You are my friends if you do what I command you. No longer do I call
you servants, for the servant does not know what his master is doing;
but I have called you friends, for all that I have heard from my Father
I have made known to you." (John 15:15)

THE PHILOSOPHER ALFRED NORTH Whitehead famously stated
that "religion runs through three stages, if it evolves to its final satisfaction: . . . the transition from God the void to God the enemy,
and from God the enemy to God the companion."[1]

John tells us that Jesus did not come into the world to judge
the world, as it was already under judgment. Rather, "God sent the
Son into the world, not to condemn the world, but that the world
might be saved through him" (John 3:17). "The true light that enlightens every man was coming into the world" (1:9). He was the
light of the world, the very logos of the world, its height and depth,
soul and wisdom, and the darkness that ground its teeth at his coming could not snuff it out.

This is metaphor, cipher, and symbolism at its best. But its
message is clear. God is love, and therein is the truth that enlightens

1. Alfred North Whitehead, *Religion in the Making* (New York: New
American Library, 1974), 16.

our hearts and dissipates the darkness. It is God's love that grounds all knowledge, illuminates understanding, and turns what we know into wisdom. For St. Augustine, who struggled so long to find God, without the love of God in our hearts and faith in Christ, there can be no true understanding of anything. It is only when we see the world through the eyes of faith that we begin to understand God's created order, his love for us, and our place in the universe. Augustine, who was both a Roman citizen and a Christian scholar, was an admirer of Plato and Aristotle. He endorsed their famous virtues of wisdom, courage, moderation, and justice, but he transformed them in a unique way. He grounded all four in God's love. The result: "*wisdom is love distinguishing between what advances* our life toward God or hinders it; *courage is love bearing all things for the sake of God; moderation is love keeping itself pure* for God; and *justice is love serving God only*."[2] He would expand this theme time and again, especially in his work *The City of God*.

John sets the stage of Jesus as Counselor-Companion. He opens us to Jesus' invitation to become his friends that we may know all that his Father cherishes for us to know, as a brotherhood and sisterhood of children of God.

≈≈≈

"Blessed are the poor in spirit, for theirs is the kingdom of heaven."
(Matt 5:3)

If your cup is already full, then nothing new can be added. Both the Old and the New Testament emphasize the humility of the heart. Even Socrates knew that wisdom requires self-emptying. We cannot be receptive to learn anything if we already claim to know everything. The Wisdom tradition of the Psalms, Proverbs, Job, and Ecclesiastes all promote the identical teaching: that the fear of the LORD is the beginning of wisdom, that humility is the antidote of inordinate pride. Even Jesus refused to count equality with God a thing to be grasped.

2. Slightly altered. See Augustine, *On the Morals of the Catholic Church*, trans. Richard Stothert, in NPNF1, ed. Philip Schaff (Peabody, MA: Hendrickson, 1994), 4:41–63.

It is so difficult to be humble, both spiritually and intellectually. We live in a culture dominated by thousands of specialists. We need them all. But each is only a part of the whole, and in the center stands God. The artist cannot say to the chemist, "I don't need you," anymore than the scientist can say to the saint, "You don't really understand, do you?"

The American philosopher John Randall Jr. argues that religion is non-cognitive and non-representative. By that he means that religious statements cannot offer any real knowledge (cognition) about the universe. Only science can do that. Nor do religious statements describe (represent) anything "out there." Yet Randall acknowledges that religious statements do express savoir-faire with respect to how to live. They provide a "vision" that encapsulates what the cognitive and representative sciences tell us.[3] Faith and reason have always been embraced by the Christian tradition. Jesus incarnated both. As our Companion, he invites us to unite the same. Faith enables us to trust in God, in God's love, and in God's presence in the world. God's gift of reason, illuminated by the mystery of transcendence, enables us to discern, probe, and weigh truth from falsehood. To be humble in spirit is a first step toward entering God's kingdom of heaven as it makes life on earth so truly worth living.

≈≈≈

"Love your enemies; do good to those who hate you;
bless those who curse you, pray for those who abuse you."
(Luke 6:27–28)

Jesus' counsel cuts straight into our hearts, piercing our egos to the core. It is so much more satisfying to hate back, to curse and offend when abused. Such instant justice salves the darker spirits of our nature. It appeases our primal instinct for revenge, for immediate redress. The urge is powerful, almost irresistible, but tragically self-destructive. For hate only begets more hate, profanity self-disgust,

---

3. See John Hicks, ed., *Classical and Contemporary Readings in the Philosophy of Religion*, 3rd ed. (Englewood Cliffs, NJ: Prentice Hall, 1990), 313–33.

and spite, feelings of helplessness and self-loathing; all of which exacerbate despair.

Have you ever become so angry as to strangle on your own rage? Only to slump into tears and helplessness, once the attack is over? Whatever sense of justification you might have derived quickly abates, only to have the hurt of the incident resurface in your heart a thousand times. It is difficult to let go, to free yourself of all the pain and simmering bitterness.

Contemporary psychologists refer to a therapy known as "radical acceptance." One accepts what has happened, seeks to understand it, then moves on. "Here is the incident, its hurt and pain. Now as I stare at it, I draw a line, here in the sand. I shall leave it here, at this line. I do not need to carry it a second longer or a synapse further. It is time to move on." All this occurs in the company of the therapist, or with the counselor's help, today's modern companion of the soul.

Jesus practiced the therapy too, if not founded it. We know it as "radical forgiveness." Love those who hate you, do good to those who curse you, and pray for those who abuse you. For, strangely, as we do, God fills our hearts with peace.

∾∾∾

"If anyone strikes you on the cheek, offer the other also....
Your reward will be great, and you will be children of the Most High;
for he is kind to the ungrateful and the wicked." (Luke 6:29–35)

Martin Buber tells the story of a rabbi and his brother who went to the House of Study to seek out another rabbi for consolation. Their problem: "Our sages have offended us with words that bring us no peace. They tell us that 'Men should praise and thank God for suffering just as much as for well-being, and receive it with the same joy.'" The rabbi listened and then laughed. "You'd better find someone else, for I've never experienced suffering." The two brothers knew that the rabbi's life had been nothing but a web of need and anguish. Then they realized the truth of the first sages' teachings: that to accept suffering with love is the only path to joy.[4]

Paul's letters know only too well of "the ungrateful and the wicked." His advice: "Avoid them!" (2 Tim 3:5). Nonetheless, he catalogs the full range of their impact on others: "In the last days distressing times will come. For people will be lovers of themselves, lovers of money, boasters, arrogant, abusive, disobedient to their parents, ungrateful, unholy, inhuman . . . lovers of pleasure rather than lovers of God, holding to the outward form of godliness but denying its power" (3:1–5). Jesus had met the same. But as he guided his disciples through their own webs of anguish, he urged them to love even those who abused them. Even Paul had to acknowledge the same: "[Love] bears all things, believes all things, hopes all things, endures all things. Love never ends" (1 Cor 13:7–8).

There was a man in the mountains who every Christmas Eve became inebriated. He would begin drinking several days in advance, and by the hour of that holy night, would be intoxicated out of his mind. He would begin by trashing all the gifts under the tree, then crush and destroy its branches and all of its lights and decorations. The children would run to their mother to huddle behind her skirts with tears in their eyes, swollen with disappointment. And so I would come down, along with his brother, to subdue the violent father until the sheriff could arrive and haul him off to jail. Later, I'd drive into town to visit the shattered prisoner. "Preacher, I know I'm sick. God knows I'm sick and God knows I need help."

Never once did his wife upbraid him. She bore his alcoholic illness, his bouts with drunkenness and abuse, with patience and, yes, with pain. She loved him and her children loved him too. Their littlest boy would often run out to greet me, and we'd gather apples together in the side yard. So too his brother agonized over his brother, and on that Night of all God's Holy Nights, together we picked through the broken glass and scattered presents. The sheriff incarcerated the father until the man could be seen by a physician, who in turn convinced him to enroll in Alcoholics Anonymous, thus launching him on the path toward eventual sobriety. Some

---

4. Buber, *Tales of the Hasidim*, 237f.

wives would have left this drunken wretch; some children would have despised such a father; some brothers refused ever again to clean up behind him. But these were mountain people, who knew what suffering meant, and in both good and bad times trusted God.

Jesus reminds us that God loves the sick and the twisted, as much as he loves each of us. And in turn, we know what God expects for each of us to do.

~.~.~

"Do not judge, and you will not be judged." (Luke 6:37a)

The wisdom of Jesus' counsel transcends debate. It hurts to acknowledge that from time to time we often judge others. Numerous factors, however, psychologically and spiritually, support Jesus' saying.

First off is the phenomenon of *projection*. We cannot help but recognize aspects of ourselves in the people we judge. "Look at that! At their behavior! How disgusting and shameful!" Their faults stand out all too well as manifestations of our own darker sorrows. Our judgment of others is really a judgment on ourselves. It alarms us, and we spring into judgment.

Second is *absolution, the need to experience forgiveness for our repressed misdeeds.* To condemn another person's actions or words assuages our consciences. It makes us feel better. "Thank heavens I've never done that! Or if I did, I was justified. God knows I'm innocent! Truly, I'm trying to be clean. I feel so much better now." There is even a twisted form of it. In German it's called *Schadenfreude*, the joy of watching one's enemies suffer.

Third is *deception*. "If we say that we have no sin, we deceive ourselves, and the truth is not in us" (1 John 1:8). In suppressing our personal sin, we become inauthentic. Sartre called it *mauvaise foi*, or "bad faith." He created whole novels and stories around people of bad faith. He wrote *No Exit* to expose those who deny their default. In truth, we become paranoid if accused of the actions and words we denounce in others. Arrogance, self-righteousness, and contempt replace the fairer virtues we so long to claim.

Finally, and ever so surely, we sink into *depression*, if not cycles of regret. "For I do not do the good I want, but the evil I do not want is what I do" (Rom 7:19). The same was true for Herod Antipas. Long after John the Baptist's arrest, the tetrarch protected him. Mark tells us he knew "he was a righteous and holy man." Then came the night of Herod's birthday and the great banquet in his honor. Salome danced. He promised her half his kingdom. Never had he felt so grandiose. Then she asked the unimaginable. The head of John the Baptist on a platter! O star of David! O Most High, what have I done?

Projection. Absolution. Deception. Depression. "Judge not," says Jesus, and you will be spared the sorrows of an ungrateful nature. Remember that God "makes his sun to rise on the evil and on the good, and sends his rain on the righteous and on the unrighteous" (Matt 5:45). Judge others? No. Rather be merciful as your Father in heaven is merciful. And leave the "judging" to God.

≈≈≈

"Do not condemn, and you will not be condemned." (Luke 6:37b)

There came to the monastery in the fall of that year a mason, whom André, our director, engaged to make repairs. The man's past was a secret. We knew nothing about him. Only André knew the man. "He has his ways, but we shall all respect him," said André. "Give him his leave; he's a good man."

His name was *Archange*! "Archangel" in English. He was short, almost diminutive, with coarse gray hair, thick white eyebrows, a fine nose and pale lips, framed within a tanned face of craggy grooves and deep lines. We could only guess at the decades of sunrises and sunsets he had witnessed, or the many seasons of summer and winter through which he had labored at his trade. His steel blue eyes missed nothing. His weathered hands and chapped fingers moved quickly as his trowel smoothed out each layer of mortar, before placing new stone upon stone. Well into winter, he refurbished the chapel, our sleeping quarters, and the long, gray walls that encompassed the estate's grounds. Alone in the evenings, he kept to himself, smoked his pipe, and stared into the flames of the grand salon's fireplace.

He had seen atrocities, escaped atrocities, if not even worse. The War was past, but not its deep etchings on his face. What family he had once enjoyed was gone. He worked from morning to evening, in the frost and the cold. When his work was completed, he rode off on a bicycle, with his trowel and small bundle of clothing strapped to his back. Before he left, André came out into the courtyard, embraced him, and kissed his neck. Where he went next, only God knows.

The student sitting opposite the professor had submitted her report—all eight to twelve pages. She had based it on the role of the *sadhu* in Hindu culture. Only, for all her research, the paper fell woefully shy of college-level quality. The professor had encircled in bright red ink the scores of syntactical and grammatical errors. They filled every page. Not even an F+ would have done justice to her effort. But the professor told himself that he was there to teach, inspire, and facilitate. Of what value would an F have been? And of what *mauvaise foi* would a passing grade have reinforced? So he did what he had learned to do after years of teaching: give her another chance before assigning a grade. She appeared stunned. "No one has ever told me I couldn't write," she said. She stared at her paper and the numerous mistakes he had circled. "I know you can bring it up to standard, if you'll try. Then I'll grade it. OK?" "Yes, sir," she answered with face bowed. She went on to graduate with honors. Three years after her graduation, she returned to the college to thank the professor and one other who had encouraged her similarly. She had come at the invitation of the college to speak in convocation and to read her prize-winning poetry to the assembled students.

Sometimes we all need a second chance and need to give others the same. For of what value is *condemnation* without an opportunity for *reclamation*? Isn't that what the Son of Galilee was all about?

≈≈≈

"Friend, who set me to be a judge or arbitrator over you?" (Luke 12:14)

The man had wanted Jesus to take sides, namely his against his brother's. Jesus' answer must have stunned the man, for it resulted in a parable, exploring and exposing our proclivity for greed. Greed is such a debilitating vice. It puts a cash value on everything, cheapening it down to a commodity. But it does so at the price of the value of our soul.

There is much to say about greed, but the text's quieter issue is our wanting Jesus to take sides, namely, ours. Jesus declined. His purpose wasn't to take sides. It still isn't. "Who made me your arbitrator?" Jesus didn't come to judge the world but to save the world. We know how disheartened Jesus became by those who judged others. That we should want to use Jesus to pass judgment on others—of course, in our favor—skews the whole purpose of God's love. "Cast the mote out of your own eye before you obsess about the speck in your brother's," is Jesus' response. It is blunt, yes, but exposes the shallowness of our souls and our need of redemptive grace.

In truth we would love for Jesus to champion our causes, solve our problems, adjudicate our disputes, defend us against our enemies, and rescue us from the debacles we create. His answer, however, gives us pause. If we are to do good to those who hate us, bless those who curse us, and pray for those who abuse us, then asking Jesus to reverse his values would be tantamount to asking Jesus to go away. It would elevate rather than eliminate a petty heart; it would maximize rather than minimize selfish pride; and rather than striving to transform our lives, we would settle for conforming them to the standards of our broken world.

Dear God, forgive us for our wanting you to do what we must do for ourselves: to love others as you love us.

~~~

"Forgive, and you will be forgiven." (Luke 6:37)

Jacob had wrestled all night with himself and God. Tomorrow he would have to face Esau. It had been so easy to trick his brother, to steal not only his father's blessing but his brother's birthright as well. Now he would be crossing back into Ephraim, the land he loved and from which he had fled some twenty years earlier. "He's coming with four hundred men," his servants warned. "We have seen their dust clouds in the sunrise and sunset. Their fires tonight are visible, even from here." So Jacob set about to meet him. Early the next morning, he crossed the Jabbok brook and placed his servant girls and their children in the first wave, Leah and her children in the second, and Rachel and Joseph in the third. With a heavy heart, he advanced alone to await his brother. Soon the horizon filled with Esau and his four hundred, their banners flapping eerily in the dry breeze. On they came, with the dust of their camels and horses rising red in spiraling clouds before them. Jacob ran forward and fell on his face. "My brother! My brother!" He could not bring himself to say, "Forgive me," for he was still too proud. But Esau reined up and dismounted, fell on his neck and kissed him, embraced him and together they wept with joy and gladness. Then, Jacob, for all his hardness of heart, could contain his emotions no longer, and weeping with remorse and unparalleled happiness, uttered from the soul of his heart, "Truly to see your face is like seeing the face of God" (Gen 33:10).

Why is forgiveness so powerful, cleansing, and redemptive? Because it mirrors the very essence of God.

≈≈≈

"Give and it will be given to you." (Luke 6:38)

It was Thanksgiving, 1947. For weeks we kept our gifts secret. Our teacher stored them in her closet as, one by one, we brought them in. Sometimes a mother would drop them off at the school's office. I brought mine in a brown paper bag and left it at the teacher's desk. It was my favorite red-and-black checkered flannel shirt. It no longer fit, as the sleeves were too short, but sometimes I wore it anyway. After all, a boy's favorite shirt is a boy's favorite shirt. My mother wanted to cut it up for cleaning rags, until the teacher sent home the note I showed her.

> Our classroom is collecting food items, coats, gloves, shirts, shoes, and any other items you can donate for the Smith family this Thanksgiving. Shirts are especially needed, as they are for a boy in our classroom whose father is out of work. Anything you can give will be greatly appreciated.

"How old is this boy?" my mom asked. "My age." "How big, tall, etc?" "About like me, Mom, except a little shorter." "Well, get that shirt of yours and any others like it. You've outgrown it anyway." "But, Mom! It's my favorite shirt." "Get it," she replied. "What's more, your teacher says she needs someone to deliver the gifts. I'm going to volunteer you to help her husband take them." So I wrapped the shirt, along with others, and helped Mom place them in a large grocery bag with other goods and food items. That Wednesday after school, I rode to the family's house with the teacher's husband. Long before we got there, the neighborhood's poverty came into view. Tiny bungalows, unpainted houses in ill repair, debris in the yards, and old cars parked in rotting leaves forewarned of what to expect. We found the house, got out, and carried the boxes to the door. The boy's mother came out, somewhat shocked, before realizing what was happening. Tears pooled in her eyes. "Those can't be for us!" she cried. "O how kind, O how good." I was afraid my classmate would see me, but he wasn't home. One by one, we unloaded all the boxes and carried them to the door. The woman continued to cry as we lined them up on her porch. "Please! It is an honor to do this," the teacher's husband said. "May God bless you," he tried to cheer her. We left with her still crying, as she pulled the boxes into her house.

Thanksgiving passed. The following Monday I returned to school. Snow had fallen and the wind was biting cold. The young boy stood by the teacher's desk, with a note to read that his mother had written. He had hung up his coat, which someone had provided, and with blushing pride was wearing my red-and-black checkered flannel shirt. It was even a little short on him. But he was so happy and proud of his new warm shirt.

I have received plenty of shirts from family and friends as the years have gone by, but none ever looked so fine on a young boy's shoulders as that red-and-black checkered flannel shirt.

∼∽∼

"You are the light of the world." (Matt 5:14)

Kenneth J. Foreman Sr., long-time editor of the *Presbyterian Outlook*, was fond of telling a story entitled, "Candles on the Glacier."

Villagers crossing between two mountains had to climb past, through, and over a dangerous glacier. Night crossings were especially perilous, so each traveler carried a candle and placed it thoughtfully along the path to guide others. Far off in the distance, the glacier glowed with its myriad light that guided the wary over the treacherous fissures. Foreman was respected and cherished for his own candles of wisdom, wit, and enlightenment, which he lit for Christian pilgrims during his stint as the magazine's theological editor. With esteem, his obituary remembers him as "A Candle on the Glacier."

Jesus asks us to be such a light. To be a bold, visible light for all to see that all may know of the Light that enlightens and guides us across life's caverns and pitfalls. You are that light, that shining star, that glowing reflection of hope in the dark that enables others to see the reflection of God's goodness in you. But that requires effort, says Jesus, by standing for what is right, doing what is right, and praying for what is good and right. For the extent to which we do transforms our lives into "candles on the glacier," too. Even the Buddha taught his disciples that a good person is "like a snowy mountain, whose brightness can be seen from afar."

Jesus seeks to comfort us, even in his teachings. A city set on a hill cannot be hidden, anymore than the goodness of God in a human life can be snuffed out by evil and darkness. Rome attempted it at Golgotha, but the goodness of God is eternal and forever superior to malice and darkness. So "let your light so shine that others may see your good works," says Jesus, "and give glory to your Father who is in heaven."

~~~

"Behold, I send you out as sheep in the midst of wolves; so be wise as serpents and innocent as doves." (Matt 10:16)

Jesus was a master of metaphor, a consummate artist when it came to inspiring insight through symbol and similitude. Wolves, serpents, sheep, doves—each in its way is an ancient archetype for revealing and concealing meaning and truth, mystery and enlightenment. Wolves and serpents are as old as primordial man, each serving as a talisman or totemic object invested with sacred lore, guarded by ritual and steeped in taboo. The modern emblem of medicine to this day still depicts Asklépios' serpent coiled about the physician's urn. Still sacred too is the Mother Wolf as tribal protector and bountiful provider. One doubts, however, that Jesus had these archetypes in mind. Wolves and serpents symbolize the more terrifying order of the fallen world, requiring God's children to be cautious, wary, perceptive, and wise; yet, gentle as sheep and innocent as doves. It is not our role to be secretive, covert, clandestine, or conniving, or to sink spiritual teeth into humanity's passersby. Wise and wary, yes; but gentle and innocent, condemning no one while loving everyone, even those who curse and abuse us. We may not succeed every time, but Jesus urges us to try.

The more we know of Jesus as Counselor-Companion, the more we need his encouragement. To be Socratic and saintly, with our eyes on God, is truly a calling worth striving to attain, thanks to the loving presence and support of the indwelling Christ.

~~~

"And the great throng heard him gladly." (Mark 12:37b)

The word in Greek is *hédéos*, an adverb, meaning "sweet," "with pleasure," "gladly," or "willingly." Bullied and beaten down by their own elders, Sanhedrin, priests, and Roman presence, the "great throng," or "populous," gladly heard Jesus, willingly savoring and deriving joy from his word. How sweet his statements rose above the din of the religious pirates who controlled access to the nation's only visible passage to the heart of God! Now Jesus has flung open that door for all to enter. "Ask, and it will be given you; seek, and you will find; knock, and it will be opened to you," says Jesus. Maybe not always in the way we want, but certainly in the way we need. "For your Father knows what you need before you ask him" (Matt 6:8b).

Even Jesus' mandates make the heart glad, for they ring with the fullness of his reassurance and love. "Take my yoke upon you and learn of me . . . for my yoke is easy and my burden is light" (Matt 11:29–30).

In the final analysis, *euangelion* means "good news." "For it is the power of God for salvation to everyone who has faith" (Rom 1:16). No wonder they heard him gladly, with joy and pleasure, willingly surrounding him that day in April, protecting him from the self-righteous bearers of the public sword.

Who among us, when cast down and bestead, has not found in Jesus that abounding joy that overcomes fear and sorrow? With hope for tomorrow and forgiveness for today, it is a joy to find respite in him. Rightly were they astonished by his teachings and admonitions, drawn to his presence like scattered sheep, responding to the voice of their Shepherd.

O Jerusalem, Jerusalem! How he longed to gather you under his wings, but you were too proud to receive him.

~~~

"I tell you, my friends . . . [are] not five sparrows sold for two pennies? And not one of them is forgotten before God." (Luke 11:4, 6)

Again we meet the word "friend" in the dative plural form of *philos*. Though we translate it "friend," it evinces a far wider range of meanings, such as "loved," "dear one," and "congenial associate." But in essence it means: "Do you not realize that God cares about you, infinitely?"

We, on the post-Classical Era side of humanity, fail sometimes to remember the levels of stratification that defined the Roman-Palestinian society of Jesus' homeland. This is not to say that contemporary levels of stratification fare better or promote a healthier environment or a more just commonwealth of equality. Class differences and prejudices haunt every society, much to the sorrow of the concerned and the poor. Nonetheless, in the face of such, Jesus reminds us that God loves us all.

In his famous *Nicomachean Ethics*, Aristotle addressed the formalities and limitations appropriate to "friendship." Basically, he identified three strata of relationships and advised accordingly: one should treat *superiors* with a dignity befitting them; *subordinates* with an eye to propriety; *equals* with a mutual respect and camaraderie. As for *servants and artisans*—a sort of fourth stratum—their usefulness to society allows us to formulate our own assessment and extent of relationship. These classifications in a variety of forms still govern our relationships and friendships to this day. In God's eyes, however, all are equal. Not a person "is forgotten before God."

I shall forever remember returning to my student apartment, elated with having passed my language exams and relishing a moment of pride. Beside me walked a fellow student who had failed his exams for a second time, thus forfeiting his quest for a PhD. As we walked along, a child ran toward us from the apartment complex. "Daddy, Daddy!" she called. As she drew closer, she held up her arms for her father to lift her into his. My heart burned with pain—for him, his future, his little girl, and for myself. He bent forward, swooped her up, kissed her little cheeks, and she kissed his.

O Father, Father! O heavenly Father! How slow we are to learn! How magnificent your equanimity, your fatherly kindness, your tender forbearance, your eternal love! O what is pride that man should deign to boast of any achievements, save your love!

~~~

"Take nothing for your journey . . ." (Luke 9:3)

It was the first time he was sending them out on their own. Their first commission! They were to "take nothing for the journey." According to Mark, the only exception was a staff, their only visible sign of support, but no bread, or bag, or money. In contrast, even the Buddha permitted his monks begging bowls. Yes, Jesus approved of sandals and a tunic, although in Luke's account, Jesus doesn't even allow them a staff. But Jesus was looking for something more. Nothing to lean on but their *faith*! Nothing to fall back on but the *good news of the gospel and its healing power*. "So they went out and preached that men should repent. And they cast out many demons, and anointed with oil many that were sick and healed them" (Mark 6:12–13).

The truth of Luke's 9:3 injunction, however, is remarkable. It mirrors an element of Zen that is worth considering. D. T. Suzuki, one of the most celebrated Zen teachers of the twentieth century, wrote:

*Religion requires something inwardly propelling, energizing, and capable of doing work. . . . Zen does this by giving one a new point of view of looking at things, a new way of appreciating the truth and beauty of life . . . by discovering a new source of energy in the inmost recesses of consciousness, and by bestowing on one a feeling of completeness and sufficiency. . . . This may be called a resurrection.*

He proceeds to offer an ancient koan by way of example:

*Empty-handed I go and yet the spade is in my hands;*
*I walk on foot, and yet on the back of an ox I am riding.*[5]

If we have Christ in our hearts, what need have we of an outward spade? Isn't his presence and love sufficient? To be certain, there are times and places for long robes, crosses and vestments, cinctures, prayers, and above all Scripture. However, there are no substitutes for God's forgiveness and love. Take nothing for the journey compels us to trust in Christ alone, that he may become that "inwardly propelling, energizing . . . new source . . . in the inmost recesses of [our] consciousness," thus bestowing on us the "feeling of completeness and sufficiency" we require to be his joyful disciples in our time.

~~~

"Take heed then how you hear; for to him who has will more be given,
and from him who has not, even what he thinks that he has
will be taken away." (Luke 8:18)

Jesus insists on confronting us with the truth about ourselves. Of what value would his love for us have been, if he had suppressed the truth concerning God's highest hopes for us? Jesus' saying above is difficult. It strikes us as so unfair, so unlike Jesus' more caring and inclusive statements. Why would anyone want to take anything away from those who have not? Are they not already suffering enough deprivation? Why deprive them of the little they have?

---

5. D. T. Suzuki, *Essays in Zen Buddhism*, 1st ser. (New York: Grove, 1961), 268, 272.

Jesus, of course, is addressing our delusions. We must lose them to become whole again. The Master Healer knows they must go. Nonetheless, we cling to them, for they are so appealing, engaging, and delectable. They are all we have, we plead with Jesus. Please don't take them away. "Must it ever be thus, that the source of our highest happiness is the fountain of our misery?" mourns the Poet, who feared losing his own delusions. No! It doesn't have to be, provided we surrender that kernel of hopelessness to which we cling. Do we even know what it is? "Let it go!" says Jesus. "Forget it and come to me!"

Conversely, the former part of his statement is reassuring and redemptive. "To him who has, more shall be given." How fragile our faith, how grave our doubts; but if our hearts are open to his, then he promises to build his kingdom of love even on our frail foundations. Indeed, the more faith we invest in him, the stronger our faith grows; the more love we shower on others, the greater that love abounds in our hearts; the more goodness, kindness, and mercy we extend to others—above all to the lonely, the poor, the miserable and bereft, and especially to our enemies—the more God's goodness, kindness, and mercy is able to shape our own lives. Such a principle of grace! Such a calculus of love!

How blunt and yet beautiful Jesus' statement is! How harrowing and healing! Provocative and whole! O LORD, test my faith of having and having not that I might have that alone which inspires and purifies my heart!

~~~

"He that is not against you is for you." (Luke 9:50)

In Hinduism the greeting is known as *namesta*. It consists in bringing together the palms of one's hands in front of one's heart, along with a light bow of the head. It is an ancient greeting and signifies: "The spirit in me greets the same spirit in you" or "The God in me greets the God in you." The latter may sound shocking at first, but we in the West, especially Christian, are to remember what the Scriptures record in Genesis: "Let us make man in our image, after our likeness. . . . So God created man in his own image . . . male and female . . . and blessed them" (Gen 1:26ff).

Our world has become multinational, multicultural, and globally one. Just as the hand cannot say to the heart, "What need have I of thee?" nor can the West say to its counterpart in the East, "What have our religious traditions to do with yours?" We have all been created in the image of God, in the likeness of God, and God's *ruah*, or inspiration, endows all humanity's earthly frame and gives it its soul.

Until I sprained my ankle, M saved a bike for me every morning in our RPM class. I would pass her husband, stepping lightly along on his treadmill, and exchange smiles, but with M it was different. She would place her palms together, by her heart, and greet me in *namesta* style. Soon, I responded with the same. Sometimes her husband and I would sit together in the lounge and exchange ideas, share our political views, and even stories about ourselves. His favorite expression: "You know, all good Hindus are capitalists." Her favorite: "I respect your tradition; and I know you respect mine." When they returned to India to visit family, we teased each other about their bringing me back a reincarnation. "Just any will do."

As Paul summarized for the Romans: "For it is not the hearers of the law who are righteous before God, but the doers of the law who will be justified. . . . [For] they show what the law requires is written on their hearts" (Rom 2:13, 15). How wise and kind Jesus was when he scolded his own that day for saying, "Master, we saw a man casting out demons in your name, and we forbade him, because he does not follow with us." Is not the name of Jesus translatable wherever goodness and love prevail?

~~~

"Do not render to dogs what is holy or cast pearls before swine."
(Matt 7:6)

Even Jesus experienced heartbreaking moments with a range of people of diverse personalities. Mark reports that in "his own country" people "took offense at him" so much so that Jesus "could do no mighty work there" (Mark 6:1–6). Luke narrates how, following his sermon in the synagogue of Nazareth, those who heard him "were filled with wrath . . . and rose up and put him out of the city" (Luke 4:28f). Matthew records a series of heart-rending judgments that Jesus felt compelled to pronounce against his own nation's leaders (Matt 23–1-36), ending in his sonorous lament: "O Jerusalem, Jerusalem! . . . Behold, your house is forsaken and desolate."

Not all of our intentions, especially our best, appeal to the unappealable, to the hardened of heart whom God in his patience alone knows best how to redeem. In those cases, says Jesus, "shake off the dust that is on your feet for a testimony against them" (Mark 6:11). It is a kind of spiritual "Enough is enough." I will not hate or abuse you as you have hated and abused me, but *enough is enough*. I leave now in peace. O borderline friend and breaker of hearts, how often we might have consoled one another and befriended each other in joy and in sorrow!

There are times when we must leave the "forsaken and desolate" to come into self-consciousness on their own, as well as discover for themselves their need of God. Until then, it is best to pray, to do good to all, and render unto no one evil for evil.

≈≈≈

"He who believes in me, as the scripture has said,
'Out of his heart shall flow rivers of living water.'" (John 7:38)

The closest texts that mirror Jesus' reference appear in Isaiah. "With joy you will draw waters from the wells of salvation" (12:3). "Ho, everyone who thirsts, come to the waters; and he who has no money, come . . ." (55:1). There is a double entendre here that speaks as much to our hearts as our requirement to speak to the hearts of others. Serving Jesus is always twofold.

In the Holston Valley of Virginia, near the historical town of Abingdon, and on one of the farms where I was reared as a boy, there gushed out of the Knobs as sweet a spring as any a man tasted. Known as the Laurel Springs, it quenched the thirst of countless passers-by, weary tenants, and woodsmen alike. How often we paused our wagons between harvests of tobacco and corn, to kneel beside its clear cold water to quell our thirsts. Earlier in the season, my aunts and cousins and I would have already visited the Springs during our forays of berry picking. With strawberry-stained fingers and thorn-bruised hands, we too would kneel beside its life-giving waters and drink our hearts' content. Sometimes we'd gather as many as twenty quarts of strawberries and later an equal number of blackberries. If not too weary, we'd carry home several pails of water too.

Of course, Jesus' point in John's passage has to do not only with God's life-giving waters sustaining us, but with God's Spirit within ourselves overflowing with love of God and love for one another. Does not part of the miracle of life reside in realizing that God not only provides for our physical thirsts, anxieties, and pleasures, but above all for our spiritual needs, sorrows, and worries, and longs with gentle heart for us to care for others?

～～～

"But a Samaritan, as he was journeying, came to where he was; and when he saw him, he had compassion . . ." (Luke 10:33)

One could call the Parable of the Good Samaritan the Parable of One Person Away. Have we not all longed for that one person who knows someone who could help us, if only that first person would mention our name, but sadly they never do? To be so close, and yet bypassed is devastating. Why couldn't that one person have mentioned our name? Why couldn't they have stopped whatever they were doing long enough to consider our credentials or potential and recommend us?

It hurts to be left behind, to come so close to success, only to be discounted. Think of the greatness that came to Joseph because that one imprisoned cupbearer remembered his name and called his attention to Pharaoh. That one lone person made all the difference in the world for Joseph's life and the future of Israel. The same might be said of David, the shepherd-boy king, who remembered the last surviving son of Saul and brought him to his table, or of how Andrew, upon meeting Jesus, hurried to tell his brother, Peter, that he had met the LORD. One could go on. There is von Staupitz, who, serving as Luther's confessor, encouraged him to read

Galatians; William Farel, who upon meeting Calvin, insisted the young humanist remain in Geneva; or the Continental Congress, remembering Washington's courage on the Monongahela, choosing him as their supreme commander.

As disappointed as you may feel, search your heart and remember those who have helped you: whether it was your mother or father, teacher or minister, professor or supervisor, physician or counselor, colleague or superior, foreman or friend, acquaintance or cousin. Maybe that one person you've needed the most hasn't shown up yet, but wherever others have, haven't they fulfilled the role of the Good Samaritan for you? Now Jesus looks for us to be that Good Samaritan, that one person away, for others. Perhaps it is our parents, our son or daughter, our colleague, boss, neighbor, or grieving friend, or someone who has tried so hard and failed, who needs us now. How long are we going to leave them in their ditch of discouragement before offering assistance and love? If you or I do not risk doing that, then we become that one person away who turned away rather than becoming a way for another's salvation and joy.

The late Balmer Kelly, professor of New Testament at Union Theological Seminary in Virginia, became that one person away for me. By sending me off to serve with André, he opened a career for me, for which I shall ever remember him. Surely there is someone for whom you are that one person away whose heart longs for you to notice and help them today.

∼∼∼

"We must work the works of him who sent me, while it is day;
night comes, when no one can work. As long as I am in the world,
I am the light of the world." (John 9:4–5)

What if we should cease to work the works of him who sent Jesus? What if throughout the day, we ignored his injunction and allowed the night to come, without extending his works of love? The night is coming, Jesus warns, when work cannot be done, when the light of day yields to the darkness and nightfall comes. "As long as I am in the world, I am the light of the world." But what if we cease to mirror his light or carry his light, so that his light cannot be seen nor fill the darkness with works of love, or works of hope, or works of peace? What if in our own time we cease to love his light and, God forbid, let it flicker, sputter, and its glowing flame die in our hearts? What then? What of ourselves? What of the world, because we chose to let it go out, and take him with it?

Have we not lived in the world long enough to know what darkness means, what darkness does, what darkness is? The night is coming. For so many across the globe, night has already swallowed them in its darkness: the darkness of hopelessness, the darkness of fear, the darkness of injustice, of loneliness, abuse, and sorrow. Only the works of God, the works of peace and love, the works of light and hope can dispel their night of darkness within and without.

LORD Jesus, Light of light, God from above, Light of love and faith and hope, take my life, my darkness too, and fill me with your power and love, that I may work the works you do and be a light for others.

≈≈≈

"You have heard that it was said, 'An eye for an eye and a tooth for a tooth.' But I say unto you ..." (Matt 5:38)

Friedrich Nietzsche's oracle concerning the "death of God" probably constitutes his most famous rejection of "herd morality," but his critical essays on nineteenth-century European morality are of greater value than one might suppose. Books like *Beyond Good and Evil*, *Thus Spake Zarathustra*, *The Gay Science*, and *The Genealogy of Morals* are still deserving of study today. He wanted to "trans-valuate all values," or re-evaluate his era's values, and move beyond their lip service to worn-out notions of good and evil. True, he denounced with vehemence Christianity's "doctrine of resentment," as he labeled it, because, in his view, it urged the weak to undermine the nobility of the strong. It made meekness a virtue. This displeased Nietzsche, as he saw meekness as a psychological cover up for envy and resentment. Ethics has to be nobler than that. In the face of "evil," one has to be bolder, more daring and novel, courageous and realistic, if what is high-minded and excellent is to prevail. Sterile notions of the past must go. Entirely new concepts are required. "New wine cannot be poured into old wine skins," he might well have quoted Jesus.

When we search our hearts, and humble ourselves before the mirror of hypocrisy, does Jesus not come to us as something of a kinder Nietzsche? Jesus' own generation's leaders recoiled at his ideas. Are not many of our own based on a past morality, more cultural and regional, habitual and unexamined, than any based on Jesus' counsel of love and forgiveness? Are we not the ones whom Jesus calls to move beyond our present views of good and evil that we may truly represent God's highest hopes for all? To trans-valuate our own values is hard to do, but with Christ's grace and presence, patience and mercy, it can be done, at least insofar as God's kingdom can come and will be done on earth as it is in heaven.

O precious God! May thy kingdom come. May thy will be done—both in and by me. May thy goodness trans-valuate all my own values and cherished principles and inform and reform my battered soul of all that is good.

∾∾∾

"And your Father who sees in secret will reward you." (Matt 6:4)

Some things require secrecy. To divulge them betrays one's heart as well as the heart of the other. Jesus was speaking about alms and prayers. To call attention to one's gift or prayer, rather than offering either out of purity of heart, borders on sacrilege. Jesus reminds us that his Father rewards us when we treasure our relationship with him more than broadcasting it for others to observe or hear, or for our ego's misguided advancement. To brag about what one does for God devaluates the self and the very core of one's relationship to God. Our love for God is for God to know, to see and observe, more than for anyone else. No words are necessary, no banners or slogans required, anymore than a lover need publicize his or her love for the beloved.

In his *Fear and Trembling*, Søren Kierkegaard explores the profound emotions that Abraham harbored as he journeyed with Isaac toward Mt. Moriah. To offer his own son tore at his senses; yet, if that's what God required—his absolute allegiance to the Absolute—then he would not waver or equivocate with God. The miracle of grace that awaited him fell equally unimagined on his soul as he journeyed back to meet Sarah. But how could he ever divulge his encounter with God? With what happened, or how it happened, or the angel that stayed his knife, or the angel's words? They were meant for his heart only. From that moment on, states Kierkegaard, something of the magnificent incommunicable descended upon the patriarch, which he could never communicate to anyone else and, therefore, in secrecy pondered the remainder of his life.

Is there a Mt. Moriah in your heart or mine where God waits to meet us in secrecy? Can we not spare him at least one absolute place where he speaks to us in privacy, where we kneel before the Absolute in silence and wonder, even in fear and trembling, where none but God may venture and we keep secret from all others? The patriarch's silent sojourn to Mt. Moriah transformed his life. It deepened his faith as no other encounter before God seems to have done. O LORD, speak to my heart as you spoke to his. Fill me with the treasure of your presence that your sacred holiness may ennoble me as your eternal grace beatified him.

# 5

# Jesus as Savior

"Behold, the Lamb of God, who takes away the sin of the world."
(John 1:29)

OUR WORLD IS UNCOMFORTABLE with the word "sin," if not cautious when employing it. In some quarters it is viewed as passé, if not ego damaging and judgmental. Thus we've replaced it with a host of more socially and psychologically acceptable terms. Realities like anger, lust, adultery, violence, revenge, self-indulgence, and spite still exist, but from a therapeutic point of view, we prefer to treat them under a miasma of disorders, diseases, and addictions. This is not to make light of depression, or bipolar and borderline disorders, or neurotic and sociopathic behavior, or drinking or eating or sexual addictions. But at some point, as individuals, we have to take claim of ourselves, if we are to become integrated and wholesome human beings again. In the language of the church, "remorse, repentance, and contrition" constitute healing steps in this process. They are inseparable from our longing for wholeness and peace.

Interestingly enough, even Buddhism grieves over a life arrested at the level of *tanha*, or craving, as it limits one to a lifetime of suffering. So too Hinduism and its concern for the attached ego that is condemned to repeat a life of materialism and pleasure, one reincarnation after another. If that's what one wants, fine! But there is so much more, the sages teach.

When our soul ponders that shining image of the imago Dei, whose essence Jesus reflects and awakens anew in our hearts, then we have to wonder with David if we too haven't "sinned and done that which is evil in God's sight" (Ps 51:4). Is it too much for each of us to sort out the secret emptiness in our lives, offer it up to God, and receive his redemptive wholeness again? Sin has been defined in many ways, but the emptiness it creates in our hearts is its best witness to our need of transformation, new vision, and love.

∼ ∼ ∼

"For the Son of man also came not to be served but to serve,
and to give his life as a ransom for many." (Mark 10:45)

Throughout history, ransoms have been required for the release of the kidnapped, abducted, and those held hostage. Always such ransoms pose risk for the redeemer, or result in the sacrifice of life for the rescuer and others. Mark's text reminds us that we are hostages in ways that only Christ can buy back, and that with his cross and life.

Close to a century ago, Dr. John Baillie, the former divine and one-time chaplain of the queen in Scotland, listed the subtle ways in which we become hostage to our self-blindness and obsessions:

> For [a] deceitful heart and crooked thoughts:
> For barbed words spoken deliberately:
> For envious and prying eyes:
> For ears that rejoice in iniquity . . . :
> For greedy hands:
> For wandering and loitering feet:
> For haughty looks . . . :
> Have mercy upon [us], O God.[1]

Baillie's column is but a tame catalog of the numerous ways in which we have allowed ourselves to become abducted from the

---

1. John Baillie, *A Diary of Private Prayer* (New York: Scribner's, 1949), 79.

family of God. One could list additional commissions, as well as heartless omissions, and still harsher acts—such as continual indifference toward God and complete absorption in the self, regardless of its cost to others.

Like the father in the story of the Prodigal, our fallen condition breaks God's heart. At the same time, our wandering natures deplete our mental and spiritual resources. The Prodigal came to his senses and returned home. God, as the waiting Father, rejoiced upon his son's homecoming, just as God awaits our own repentance and return.

~~~

"I came that they may have life, and have it abundantly." (John 10:10)

Perhaps nothing attests more powerfully to our need of God than our sense of moral despair or the presence of the void within. King David, Augustine, Matthew Arnold, and others have all decried that loneliest loneliness that lies disconsolate at the bottom of our soul. In more modern times, few have expressed it more eloquently than Goethe in his novel of the young Werther and his self-immolating sorrow:

> And what is man—that boastful demigod? Do not his powers fail when he most requires their use? And whether he soar in joy or sink in sorrow, is not his career in both inevitably arrested? And whilst he fondly dreams that he is grasping at infinity, does he not feel compelled to return to a consciousness of his cold, monotonous existence?

Or again:

> What is the destiny of man, but to fill up the measure of his sufferings, and to drink his allotted cup of bitterness?[2]

Jesus stirred human hearts with his love, his extended touch, his words of comfort and reassurance. He brought hope where

---

2. Johann von Wolfgang Goethe, *The Sorrows of Werther* (New York: Dodge, n.d.), 239 and 223, respectively.

none existed, kindness where only bitterness had prevailed; insight where glum and despair ruled. In him was life, which he shared with abundance. In his goodness, others found hope; in his mercy, courage; in his eyes on God, their own renewal and joy; in his sufferings and sorrow, redemption and life anew. For it is in losing our own life that we find it, in shouldering his cross that we become strong, in sharing his kindness that we are flooded with peace and joy. For insofar as we love, we receive love; and insofar as we forgive, we are redeemed and forgiven.

≈≈≈

"Do not be astonished that I said to you,
you must be born from above." (John 3:7b)

John presents Nicodemus as puzzled at first, perhaps not so much slow on the uptake, but hesitant to draw the feared conclusion. On the contrary, however, the Nicodemus in each of us grasps the Savior's implication immediately.

John steals into our guarded consciousness with deft metaphors, describing the elder Pharisee as a "leader," who seeks the Master under the cover of "night," to pose his overarching question, in the fear that his hunch might just be right. "For no one can do these signs apart from the presence of God." Was he not in essence saying, "Lo, if necessary, Master, I can be discrete; it can be our secret, just between us." Later, Nicodemus would plead for Jesus, at least, to receive a fair trial. "Does not our law permit him to speak in his own defense?" (John 7:50.). And at Golgotha, on that cruel night as the first stars of the Sabbath broke through the crimson dusk, we find him helping Joseph of Arimathea wrap the Master's corpse in the scented bolts of perfumed linen he provided from his own purse.

No doubt Jesus loved him; won him to his heart, respected him as a son would esteem his own father. Yet Jesus pressed him with the truth. We cannot enter the kingdom of God as if nothing needs to change in our hearts. "Do not be astonished that your whole life must be transformed," says Jesus, "born anew, born from above, seized by the grace of God, infused with God's indwelling

Spirit, if we are to become his new creation, empowered with His love and might."

We can go on being his secret admirers, if we wish, mulling over the Gospel stories and cherishing them for ourselves, whether at dawn, twilight, or dusk. But the Savior who longs to redeem us wants so much more.

∿∿∿

"Again, the kingdom of heaven is like a merchant in search
of fine pearls; on finding one pearl of great value, he went and sold
all that he had and bought it." (Matt 13:45–46)

In so many respects, life is a pilgrimage, a journey, a quest. It is a search for "that than which none greater can be conceived," for that in the light of which all else is valued. Pleasure, fame, wealth, and power have all been sought in turn. But none represents the "that than which none greater can be conceived."

Our text is not a merchant's tale, or romance, or story of tinkling caravans, or even a parable about cherished objects of affection, aesthetics, or Keat's sublime- "Ode to a Grecian Urn."

*A thing of beauty is a joy forever.*

No. It is about us, and that alone which quenches the soul's thirst. It is about our quest for God, our longing for "that than which none greater can be conceived." It is about God, in whose hands alone we find the Pearl of All Value, of "which none greater can be conceived." Thus, Jesus' story is ultimately about our conscience, its awakening, our conversion, and the reformation of our life.

∿∿∿

As he walked along, he saw a man blind from birth. His disciples asked
him, "Rabbi, who sinned . . . that he was born blind? Jesus answered,
"Neither this man nor his parents sinned; he was born blind so that
God's works might be revealed in him. (John 9:1–3)

The truth that we are born blind in order that the works of God might become manifest in us may seem strange at first, but not if you reflect on the truth about yourself. Note that Jesus does not attribute the man's blindness to sin. Rather, the human condition from birth is vulnerable, precarious, fragile, and susceptible to error and folly, until the grace of God enlightens and cleanses the heart. It is much like Plato's Allegory of the Cave. There, deep in the earth and surrounded by darkness, its chained captives groped about, struggling to make sense of life. Dancing on the cave's walls in front of them wavered figures and shadows, images and distortions, cast by the pale light of a fire's flames flickering behind them. O how adept they became at identifying the shadows. But it was not until a compassionate visitor, seeing how blind they were, unshackled one of the captives and "dragged" him into the light that the captive realized how blind he had been.

So too are we blind and susceptible, mistaking shadows and images of old prejudices and comfortable beliefs for the truth that could set us free. But, first, we have to acknowledge our blindness—however painful the process—and be led toward the light before we can realize how blind we've been. Paul said he was not ashamed of the gospel because of its power to open our eyes to the light of God's goodness and grace. Till then, we remain like Plato's captives, chained to the walls of life's cave, until God's Son descends down the dark steps of our soul to lead us back to God again.

≈≈≈

"For God so loved the world that he gave his only begotten Son ..."
(John 3:16)

That Christmas at Villemétrie André chose as his vesper text Isaiah 9:6: "For unto us a child is born, a son is given; . . . and his name shall be called Wonderful Counselor, the Mighty God, Everlasting Father, Prince of Peace." André who had no son and who had been an itinerant evangelist following World War II, stood quietly in front of the chapel's Communion table, facing us. With hands out-stretched and elements of the broken loaf in each palm, he invited us to break bread with him. "Here is his Son," said André. "*Voici son Fils. Cassé pour toi,*" he personalized the *"vous"* for each of us. "Sometimes a son is given to couples who bear no children, but on this night of holy nights, God gives his Son to each of us anew." André went on to speak additional words, but my heart was clinging to *Voici son fils,* "Here is his Son."

Friedrich Schleiermacher, a German theologian of the Great Enlightenment, explained salvation in this way:

> Our relationship to God is really an affair of the quiescent self-consciousness, looking at itself . . . and finding a consciousness of God included there. Now we know that only one relationship to the divine holiness and righteousness is proper to the corporate life of sinfulness, namely, the self-consciousness of guilt and merited punishment. [But] this must vanish at the very beginning of living . . . with Christ [our Redeemer].[3]

Brother André shied away from theological explanations. That night, Christ was so apparent in his heart as to awaken our "quiescent self-consciousness." This was true of both our corporate and individual longings for God; our longing for his Son, the Prince of Peace, symbolized in the broken elements in André's hands. "Behold! God's Son!"

❦

"Martha, Martha, you are worried and distracted by many things. Mary has chosen the better part, which will not be taken away from her." (Luke10: 41–42)

She had a sister named Mary, who sat at the LORD's feet and listened to his every word, and that with all her heart, while Martha worked tirelessly, if not without inward hurt to host the proudest guest they had ever known. "LORD, do you not care that my sister has left me to do all the work by myself?" It was such a natural question, so obvious to all. Surely Jesus understood and would favor her request! But his answer sank to the bottom of her heart. "O Martha,

---

3. Friedrich Schleiermacher, *The Christian Faith* (New York: Harper, 1956), 2:478–79.

how many distractions must we suffer before we discover the one thing that is more precious than all?" Yes, our lives are driven by a plethora of expedient distractions and many more that are equally urgent, but only one is "the better part" that cannot "be taken away." Paul Tillich called it "ultimate concern"; Anselm, "that than which none greater can be conceived"; Schleiermacher, "the feeling of absolute dependence of the finite on the Infinite"; Goethe, "that which alone is indispensable—love." Or yet again: "What is the world to our hearts without love?" Our text puts it simply: "What is the world to our hearts without redemption?"

As distractions come and go, with all our trials and wounds that unsettle the soul, there remains one joy above all others, and that is God's Son, in all his redemptive tenderness and conscience-freeing love.

≈'≈'≈

"When the days drew near for him to be taken up,
he set his face to go to Jerusalem." (Luke 9:51)

The shadow of the cross falls often upon us, visibly, and throughout the landscape of Luke's Gospel, nor should we be surprised. Jerusalem was always there in the hollow of Jesus' thoughts. He knew his destiny. How early? We shall never know. But he knew his history and the history of his beloved nation's city, and how its kings and rulers had mocked its prophets, from the time of David forward. If the past had mocked its greatest *nabiim*, why would its rulers not mock him? Still, "he set his face to go to Jerusalem." After all, the City of David was Judah's proudest crown and *terminus ad quem* of all the annual pilgrimages. Going there created elation and sorrow; stirred both national and private hopes; longings for justice and redemption, repentance and forgiveness, joy and peace of heart. Were not the great Songs of Ascent embedded indelibly in every Jewish mind and soul?

Pilgrimages have always been part of our human story, our personal and collective journeys. Our quests for the holy, for those sacred sites of *hierophanies*, where angels descend for God to mend our sorrows and rekindle our commissions, are endemic to the

process of salvation and wholeness. With resolve Jesus set his face
to go to Jerusalem, to his inexorable axis mundi, to prepare his heart
for his final pilgrimage on earth. Why should we think ourselves
exempt from the same journeys that strengthen faith?

His pilgrimage to Jerusalem invariably sweeps us along. For
we too need to find again God's holy center, God's sacred presence,
anchored in our hearts—his burning bush and Mt. Moriah—where
on our bended knees with contrite heart God lifts us to himself
anew.

~~~

"Truly I tell you, one of you will betray me...." They began
to be distressed and to say to him one after the other, "Surely, not I?"
(Mark 14:18–10)

In her article "Psychological Effects of Betrayal," Gina Scott, pop
culture and health issues expert, presents a fivefold sequence of
feelings experienced by the betrayed. Interestingly enough, the
sequence applies to the betrayer as well. She lists them as: shock,
anger, grief, isolation, and sadness. She notes that sometimes anger turns into desire for revenge, and sadness, if not treated, into
depression.[4]

As one soon to be betrayed, the Gospels depict Jesus as un-
fazed by shock or anger, yet not untouched by grief, isolation, and,
later, sadness. His grief was apparent the evening of the Last Supper.
"With desire have I desired to eat this Passover with you before I
suffer" (Luke 22:15). His isolation followed in the Garden of Gethsemane, along with premonitions of abandonment and sadness: "If
it be possible, Father, remove this cup from me." Then his words
from the cross: "My God, my God, why hast thou forsaken me?"

We seldom think of Christ as one who suffered emotional feelings. After all, wasn't he the Word incarnate, God with us? Who
neither slumbers nor sleeps? Whose capacity to endure all things

---

4. Gina Scott, "Psychological Effects of Betrayal," online: http://www.ehow
.com/info_8511243_psychological-effects-betrayal.html. See also her books
on the subject.

surpasses our understanding? The temptation to think so was condemned as early as possible by those who knew him and by the church whose creeds preserved his humanity, in all its suffering.

The central betrayers at table that night were Judas, and later, Peter, the Rock on whom Jesus would found his church. The one hanged himself after Jesus' arrest; the other wept in shame with all his soul. We may not identify ourselves with Judas, but it's impossible not to see ourselves in Peter, or commiserate with the Twelve as each asked in turn, "Is it I?" Without anger or shock, Jesus remained faithful to them. His heart even went out to Judas, if not love. "What you are about to do, do quickly."

The fivefold sequence of betrayal is something we too must live with, acknowledge, and address. Shock, self-loathing, remorse, inner flight, isolation, sadness, and shame are facets of our pilgrimage too. Jesus did not condemn his Twelve. With desire, he desired to eat the Passover with them before he suffered, before he went to his cross for them, his nation, mankind, and for each of us.

O LORD, receive our cup of betrayal into your hands that we too might be forgiven and born anew by your eternal love.

~·~·~

And he took a cup, and when he had given thanks he gave it to them,
saying, "Drink of it, all of you; for this is my blood of the covenant,
which is poured out . . . for the forgiveness of sins." (Matt 26:27–28)

The quest for the Holy Grail, and the legends attached to it, have long captured human interests, at least since the time of Sir. Thomas Mallory's inimitable *La Morte d'Arthur*. But what is its secret that it so binds itself to our hearts and stirs our restless spirits? Aside from the nails and the myriad splinters of the cross, no holy relic of higher spiritual value exists. To behold the Grail and to feel it in one's hands would flood the soul with tears of joy enough to fill the cup. What are the curly locks of Napoleon in comparison? Or even the Liberty Bell? The Magna Carta, Michelangelo's David, or the pyramids of Egypt? Sir Mallory tells us that Lancelot's long quest finally brought him to the castle gates, whereupon his request to behold the Sangreal was granted. The chamber doors flung open, and there before him on a table of silver, surrounded by four angels, glowed the Holy Grail, flooding and burning his eyes with a light he was required to endure for days. It was only with patience and diligence that his servants finally awakened him from his dream-like coma. In some accounts, he took Communion afterwards along with his knights. In others, Christ suddenly appears in the Grail and offers the cup to him. "Drink of it, my son." In Bulfinch's story, the brave knight's servants speak as follows: "Sir, the quest of the Sangreal is achieved now in you, and never shall ye see more of it than ye have seen."[5]

Where else, save in ourselves, can Christ's pure grace flood our hearts with love and salvation? Is not the Sangreal now in us? We will not find it under a dome of glass or in an ornate chest or on a pedestal mounted in some museum far away. It is something to ponder when next we kneel to take Communion or receive the holy Eucharist. "Here, LORD, am I. Fill me with your holy love and grace that I may love and tend your servants too."

∾∾∾

"A little while and you will see me no more." (John 16:16)

The philosopher Martin Heidegger writes of God's withdrawal from the world. He traces contemporary mankind's sense of loneliness back to the period of Greco-Roman mystery religions and the death of their rewarding, salvation cults. He includes Christianity in this mix. Now we live in a "destitute time," as his favorite poet Hölderlin dubs it. It all has to do with "time" and Höldlerlin's meaning of time, says Heidegger. "Ever since the 'united three'—Heracles, Dionysos, and Christ—have left the world, the evening of the world's age has been declining toward its night."[6] No god any longer gathers humanity unto himself. Truly God has withdrawn, and the night of

5. Thomas Bulfinch, *Bulfinch's Mythology* (New York: Modern Library, 1934), 415.

6. Martin Heidegger, *Poetry, Language, Thought*, trans. Albert Hofstadter (New York: Harper & Row, 1971), 89.

the world has fallen upon us. Alone and destitute, we have been left on our own.

In truth, Jesus was on the eve of his own withdrawal—from the world as well as from his disciples. Never again would they see him the same, though they would come to see him in a different light. On that Passover eve, however, the night of the world crept out of its cage and waited for Judas' departure. That Jesus felt his own decline into the night of the world's darkness is recorded in all four Gospels. "In a little while you will see me no more" puzzled them, yet the night of their own decline was descending upon them faster than they could know. With Christ's withdrawal, the whole world would soon be thrown into darkness. In Heidegger's mind, we have yet to ascend out of it, which is why both his time and ours remains "destitute." The light of the world was gone, and still is for Heidegger.

It is instructive to note, however, that the Greek word for "a little while" carries a unique meaning of "time." Yes, it is a destitute time, but only for a "*micron*." The New Testament writers utilized three words for time: *kairos*, *chronos*, and *micron*. *Chronos* refers to linear time; *kairos* to that unique moment that illuminates all other moments of time; *micron* appears and vanishes in a flash, in a heartbeat when measured against the long eons of chronological time and mankind's sojourn upon the earth.

"In a little while, you will see me again," explained Jesus (Matt 16:16). But we do so with the eyes of faith. In the long run, we must each ask our heart: "Are you still lost in the time of Jesus' withdrawal, or have you leapt with joy at the sight of his post-*micro* appearance in the hearts and souls of all who love, trust, and believe in him, worldwide?"

~~~

So Pilate, . . . having scourged Jesus, he delivered him to be crucified. And the soldiers led him inside the palace. . . . And they clothed him in a purple cloak, and plaiting a crown of thorns they put it on him. . . . And they struck his head . . . and spat upon him." (Mark 15:15–19)

Over the years, various theories of atonement have surfaced to illuminate mankind's estrangement from God, along with God's initiative to overcome that estrangement through unparalleled divine grace. At its center stands the cross. Luke favored a ransom theory; John, a death and rebirth of the soul; Paul, a vicarious expiation of all that is dark and fallen—"for while we were yet sinners, Christ died for the ungodly"; Anselm, a divine-human descent for the restoration of God's honor and humanity's salvation. Does it matter, however, which of the theories we embrace as long as our sinful hearts find wholeness and forgiveness?

In many respects, Jungian analysis provides what dogma cannot articulate. In Jungian parlance, the cross symbolizes our liberation from the dark powers of the subconscious and their incarceration of the conscious in our struggle to become whole. With its symbolism of the healing quadrant, the cross makes visible the unconditional grace of God. The wounds of the Christ are the wounds of mankind, the wounds of a torn and divided self, and yet the wounds of God—God reaching down to earth and man reaching back in the crucified hands of Jesus to receive forgiveness. In the final analysis, love is what innerves the cross. For "God is love," writes John, and the cross is that sacred place where God chose to manifest his redemptive love for each of us. For there can be no atonement of a divided subconscious self shy of its crucifixion and resurrection to new life.

The cross tells the story of Everyman. By means of it, the Gospels confront us with the truth about our obstinate and dysfunctional self. In his sufferings and crucifixion, Christ offers our broken humanity the highest and holiest powers of hope and healing. Until in faith we own that death with him—even his descent into hell—we remain strangers to God's most precious gift of all.

# 6

## Jesus as Risen

"Why do you seek the living among the dead?" (Luke 24:5)

THE WOMEN WHO CAME to his tomb that morning arrived with spices with which to bathe his body in a manner fitting of the dead. Little did they anticipate an empty grave.

While staying at the American School of Oriental Research, which at that time was located in the Jordanian quarter of Jerusalem, a visiting guest and I decided to visit Gordon's Calvary (a hillock that looks like a skull) and a nearby tomb site that seemed to fit the Gospels' descriptions of Jesus' burial place. I was young, a student, in search of my soul; the guest, an older gentleman on pilgrimage in gratitude to God. Together we wiled away sufficient afternoons, taking tea in the school's magnificent oleander-shaded garden. Gordon's Golgotha was quite convincing, but the nearby gravesite, drenched in noonday sunlight, created a hollowness within. As we stared past its hewn entrance, the retired gentleman quipped with a smile: "I don't know why we came here, because we knew it'd be empty from the start."

There is an emptiness about the human condition that only the living Christ can fill. It is that space that God has always claimed for himself, reserved for his Spirit and his risen Son. Therefore, we shall not find him in an ossuary or sunken grave. No monument encases his remains, or preserves his leached bones, nor even a fleck of his ashes. "He is risen! You will not find him here," proclaims the angel. Rather, you will find him in your heart, in the Galilee of your soul, along the shores of your thoughts and the neural pathways of your journeying, wherever you go, wherever you are, whenever you long and pray for his presence. "For lo, I am with you always," he assured his own, as his angel reassures us. "He is going before you," said the angel. "Hurry now! Pick up your pace and follow him."

~~~

"Woman, why are you weeping?" (John 20:15)

She had remained behind at the tomb. Both Peter and the "beloved disciple," whose identity John conceals from us for all time, had run to the tomb on Mary's word of discovering its emptiness. Now she was once again alone. It was the hour of her *loneliest loneliness,* the season of her own abandonment, so similar to his, to the Jesus whom she loved. "Sir, if you have taken him away, tell me where you have laid him, and I will take him away." O the hurt she must have felt! The crushing burden of having lost that singular one her heart would never forget. Her love for him; his love for her! Why? O why? O God, why him? O LORD! Why, why? She stood there, sobbing, John tells us, just as others must have sobbed at the foot of his bier, too. Yes, we should sob, even we, who stand with her in the garden, benumbed and dazed by God's Son's death and now his pillaged and vandalized tomb. Have we no understanding, nor empathy of the magnitude of their grief? Theirs was no dream or myth! Nor a tale babbled by some mendicant mystic in his hour of "cold, monotonous existence"!

There is a weeping that transcends the wail of tears. Mothers know it when they collapse beside the graves of their sons, their life-long partner husbands, and those who journeyed with them across the years. Do we not understand the merciless and callous loss the heart endures when death snares our loved ones away? My God, my God, why hast thou forsaken me? Yes, God, why?

In my book *In Praise of Virtue*, I describe what I call "moral despair." I base it on the second beatitude: "Blessed are they who mourn, for they shall be comforted" (Matt 5:4). In Greek, the word for "mourn" is *pentheo*. Quite simply, it has to do with life's unmitigated sorrow that plunges us toward despair. But once adopted as an inescapable facet of our human condition, that despair soon casts us downward into a hellish spiral, ending in what Sartre called "the death of the soul." Only faith, hope, and love can resist it and reverse life's sickness unto death. The existentialist writer Albert Camus also addressed *pentheo* in his *Myth of Sisyphus and Other Essays*. In Camus' mind, modern man will never find consolation short of embracing life's absurdity. We long for meaning, but life contains no meaning, nor is there a "meaning giver," apart from the disconsolate self—or so Camus held. Indeed, such moral despair leaves us little less than mortal mirrors of a Prometheus bound, on whom the gods' voracious vultures devour our hearts anew each day. Such is the way of moral despair.

The good news of the gospel, however, shatters this despair. The risen Christ will have none of this! Behold, the angel's words, "Why seek ye the living among the dead?" and Jesus' response to Mary's tears, "Woman, why are you weeping?" Both statements call us to trust in the transcendent reality of the living Christ and his transforming grace. "Lo, death where is thy sting? O grave where is thy victory? O tomb, thy silent triumph?" No, Mary, you will not find him here, or in any empty tomb, but his living presence reigns wherever you let him in and invite his love to conquer your heart.

≈≈≈

"And this is eternal life, that they may know you, the only true God, and Jesus Christ whom you have sent." (John 17:3)

John saw in Jesus what so few others saw, even before his death and resurrection: that to know him and to see him, to trust, believe, and love him, was to know God and receive God—*now*. It meant the eternal was present now; that the kingdom is here, not just a future event, though its consummation may still be as distant as the most far-off star. "Thy kingdom come, thy will be done, on earth as it is in heaven" is a sacred and sufficient condition for truth and goodness to prevail—now! "Father, the hour has come . . . to give *eternal life* to all whom you have given [me]" (17:1–2).

Theologians refer to John's *zoén aionion* as the "eternal now." Yes, it is mystical and spiritual, noetic and incarnate, poetic and neural, all at the same time. As Jesus went on to explain, "As you, Father, are in me and I am in you, may they also be in us, . . . so that they may be one, as we are one, I in them and you in me" (17:21–23). Jesus was talking about the present, not just about some distant time in the future, when he would join them anew in his Father's house of many mansions.

As I got off the bus near Nablus that afternoon, I shall never forget what happened. Our bus had been stopped along the way, between Jerusalem and that ancient square into which I was just then staring. Jordanian police had pulled the bus over, bordered it, and required me to produce my passport. I had none, as the consulate's office on the Israeli side of the border had warned me to hide it, since it bore the state of Israel's entrance stamp. I would not be allowed into Jordan if authorities saw it, so I was advised. Thus, the consulate's office provided me with an affidavit, confirming me as an American citizen, traveling abroad. The Jordanian police studied it, stared at me, but allowed our bus to pass on. As I glanced about the square, I noted how filled it was with silent, suspicious, and sullen men. Were they about to do what the police could not do? Had word of my arrival already spread? I paused. Perhaps my heart skipped a beat; I don't remember. I was afraid, yet not afraid, as an ineffable peace came over me; it came down and gathered me up in its angelic arms, as if God himself were present. Call it an epiphany, a young man's fancy, a childlike trust in God; but whichever it was, I experienced the *eternal now* as I stepped down. Nothing has ever happened to change or dim the memory or intensity of that moment.

Yes, it was deeply personal, a private *hierophany*, an event that rarely occurs for most of us. But faith in God and his risen Son floods the present with eternity. It fills it with the radiant and dazzling presence of all that is good and noble, and of all that is worthy of our utmost devotion. It calls us to a duty that transcends our despair, along with the cold monotonous moments of our darker hours. Yes, the eternal *is* now. Yes, the hour has come for us to be glorified in all the daily and mundane rounds of our lives, that we might show forth the goodness of God, who turns death into life and fear into joy.

~~~

"Truly I tell you, just as you did it unto the least of these my brothers, you did unto me." (Matt 25:40)

Watching the crying man weeping in the rain tore at our hearts, as we stared from our hotel window. He was seated on a bench, waiting for a bus. His black hair dripped with rain; his overcoat scarcely covered his shivering body; his sockless feet glistened wet and cold in his untied shoes. In fact, they had no shoestrings. In his hands he clutched a crumpled newspaper, protecting a piece of bread he had found somewhere. "You must give him something; you must help him," my wife whispered with tears in her eyes. I let the curtain drop, donned my coat and cap, and hurried down stairs, but when I reached the street, the homeless man was gone. Only his soggy newspaper remained where his emaciated frame had wept earlier. What if he were the Christ and I had let him go alone into the darkening night!

The eternal is now. Every moment is an opportunity to befriend and comfort the Christ in our brothers and lonely sisters. Christ is in us now. He and his Father are one, just as we are one with the Father and the Son. We are his hands now, his fingers on the broken loaves, his palms about the cup of hope and love.

"In as much as you do it to the least of these my brothers," says Jesus, "you do it unto me. In as much as you care for the least of these my sisters, you care for me. And in as much as you welcome the least of mankind's strangers, you validate the Eternal in yourself and me."

In her book *The Human Condition*, Hannah Arendt reminds us of the essential distinction between "immortality" and the "eternal." The Greeks longed for immortality, but the cycles of life— birth, youth, old age, and the grave— make immortality impossible. We are simply mortal. But eternity is different. Drawing upon the teachings of Augustine, she notes that the question "*What* is man?" is answered by our mortality, but the question "*Who* is man?" can only be answered by God. For it is he who lifts our mortality into his eternity and fulfills what our mortal natures cannot.[7]

∾∾∾

"In my Father's house are many mansions." (John 14:2 KJV)

Jesus knew so well how to comfort his disciples; and John how precious his words would become for us. We are hardly the first, however, to ponder the question, "Is there another life that we shall know?" The tombs of Ice Age humankind witness to the quandary, reflected in the gifts and weapons laid so lovingly beside the hardened bones. So too the elaborate rooms of the mummified pharaohs, inscribed with faded murals of the deceased's loving entourage, bearing urns of food and raiment and all the luxuriant comforts their passing lords might need. Socrates posed the question too: "either death is a state of utter unconsciousness or . . . a migration of the soul from this world to another." If the former, what harm could it bring, as eternity would be but "a single night"? But if the latter, then what an incomparable gain! To converse with Orpheus, Hesiod, and Homer, or with the great heroes of the Trojan War, would be an immense joy for him, as it would allow for a continuing quest of what is true and good! He drank his cup without wavering, just as Jesus drank his on the eve of his death. Both trusted in the goodness of God, each in his own way: Socrates in the form of Plato's philosophically purified Zeus; Jesus in Abba, his Father, into whose hands he committed his Spirit without further murmur, question, or dispute.

Where do you stand? Where do I stand? Our modern understanding of human physiology cannot imagine a conscious life apart from a living brain. Once it goes, doesn't consciousness go with it? We cannot expect science to answer the question for us. Yet even science fascinates us with its exploration of the internal makings of our DNA and its inseparable connection with the matrix

7. Hannah Arendt, *The Human Condition*, 2nd ed. (Chicago: University of Chicago Press, 1998), 10–21.

of the evolving universe, in all its interconnectedness, continuity, and atomic and subatomic elemental nature, reaching back to the birth of the universe and the glory of the first stars. We are the living manifestation of that gigantic burst, when God so wonderfully said, "Let there be light!" And God saw the light and pronounced it "good."

We do not have to face death with fear, no more than life without faith, hope, and love. "He who believes in me," says Jesus, "though he die, yet shall he live" (John 11:25). The afternoon before my mother died, she asked me to come to her bedside. She had been in the hospital a week. "Yes, Mom." I rose and stood at the foot of her bed. "Bennie, are my feet cold yet?" she asked. Mom never shied away from the truth. Jesus would have loved her. Of that, I have no doubt. I placed my hands on the sheet covering her feet. They were cold as ice. "You're fine, Mom," I said, as I held them in my hands, knowing the hour of her glorification was drawing near, and that soon she'd be in Another's hands.

O Father! Why do we doubt your eternal goodness, your fatherly care, your loving presence in life and death?

≈≈≈

"Receive the holy Spirit. If you forgive the sins of any, they are forgiven; and if you retain the sins of any, they are retained." (John 22b-23)

It is the risen Jesus who encourages us to act thusly. The eternal now enjoins more than enjoying Christ's warm, personal presence. Yes, he is risen to comfort us, but also to remind us of his Father's eternal love. Indeed, sins are retained unless we are willing to forgive those who hurt us. If not, they fester and swell in our souls to torment us in our loneliest loneliness. They hurt those whom we refuse to forgive as well, especially if they have any heart at all. No one is immune to unforgiven sin. There may be an occasional psychopath or sociopath without a hint of conscience, but most of us suffer from the "slings and arrows" of others, or regret those we have hurled back in moments of anger and sorrow. The offices of countless chaplains, physicians, counselors, psychiatrists, and psychologists are filled with those whose sins have been retained. Just as many, if not more, are crowded by those who refuse to forgive at all.

"Receive the Holy Spirit," said Jesus. Therein is the clue, isn't it? For without his Spirit, we are still lost in our own bound and retained sins. It doesn't have to be that way, says Jesus. Receive the Holy Spirit and forgive the sins of those whose faults have been retained far, far too long.

∿∿∿

"O men of Galilee, why stand ye gazing into heaven?" (Acts 1:11)

Could there be a more appropriate, penultimate text on which to bring our reflections to a close? "Why do you stand gawking into heaven?" the angels asked. To be certain, his disciples hated to break off. Could he not linger another fortnight, or postpone his ascension until the festival of Pentecost had passed? Was the latter not the commemoration of the giving of the Law? Why did he have to leave now, to ascend to his Father when they needed him on earth?

They were as fearful as we are, if not still immured in their grief and shock. We too fear the departure of the pre-Easter Jesus, the Comforter and Healer, whose words speak so tenderly to our burdened hearts and whose presence mends our traumatized souls. Please, don't leave us, Master. Remain beside us, whate're befall.

It's as if we've never heard of the eternal now. Poor Paul had to boost his own followers, members of his scattered tiny churches and recipients of his faithful letters, to remember the same. "For neither death nor life . . . can separate us from the love of God that is in Christ Jesus" (Rom 8:38–39). "What then are we to say? If God is for us, who can be against us?"

Somehow God's angels always know best. They knew how to comfort Jacob in his flight from Esau, to hold Moses' arms aloft above the roaring waters, to steady Samson's hands against the columns of the Philistines' pagan temple. They sang on the night of Jesus' birth, ministered to him following his trial in the wilderness, strengthened Simon of Cyrene to shoulder Jesus' cross, and, in the mists of that first Easter morning, rolled death's heaviest stone from Jesus' tomb.

"You will be endowed with God's Holy Spirit," the angels encouraged them. "You will know what to say and how to say it, and what to do and how to do it, if only you will let God into your lives. Then your mortality will shine with his eternity and you will truly become his light of the world. Come now, grasp his hand, take up your cross, and follow him."

~~~

One of the criminals who were hanged railed at him, saying,
"Are you not the Christ? Save yourself and us!" But the other rebuked
him, saying . . . "Jesus, remember me when you come in your kingly
power." And [Jesus] said to him, "Truly, I say to you, today
you will be with me in Paradise." (Luke 23:39–43)

Now we have come to that moment of moments that shall forever define the undefinable in our souls. "Remember me, LORD, when you come in your kingdom." "Truly, I say to you, today you shall be with me in Paradise."

No branch of Christianity has fathomed the mystical and spiritual reality of Jesus' reply to the dying penitent's request as profoundly as the Eastern Orthodox Church. In its funereal incantation, "Eternal is the memory of God," we are lifted into God's eternal presence, while at the same time God's eternal comfort is brought down into our earthly hearts. To be eternally in memory of God, and for God to be in eternal memory of us, has the power to transform our lives as few other acts of faith can.

As the late Donald Sheehan explains, "'to be remembered' by the LORD is the same as 'to be in Paradise.' 'To be in Paradise' is to be in eternal memory and, consequently, to have eternal existence and therefore an eternal memory of God. Without remembrance of God we die, but our remembrance of God is possible only through God's remembrance of us."[8]

8. Donald Sheehan, "Dostoevsky and Memory Eternal: An Eastern Orthodox Approach to the Brothers Karamazov," online: http://www.dartmouth.edu/~karamazov/resources/?page_id=446.

In truth, "eternal is the memory of God" means that our identity as a unique soul remains secure forever in God. It means that, though we are finite and mortal, we are nonetheless irreplaceable and non-redundant; each of us is unlike any other creation God carries in his heart. Hence, we cannot cease to be or somehow unbecome, since we are in his memory eternally. Conversely, in the same manner is our memory of God: the ineffable, the irreplaceable, the "that than which none higher can be conceived," without whose Being we would cease to exist. His eternity flows into us, as our mystery and destiny are hidden in God. By letting God be God in our lives, his eternal love and kingly power renew our hearts every day. Instead of wrong, there can be right; instead of evil, good; instead of anger, forgiveness; instead of remorse, peace; instead of despair, hope; instead of hell, paradise; instead of death, eternity in God.

"Remember me when you come in your kingdom" is a daily prayer to cherish every day for the rest of our life. But "Will I live again?" you might ask. "I mean, with him in heaven?" you might press. To which the Christ and Gospels reply: "Yes. Yes, dear soul! Yes. For your heart is already with me in the Paradise of God's soul."[9]

9. For more on the afterlife, see Charles Hartshorne, *Omnipotence and Other Theological Mistakes* (Albany, NY: SUNY Press, 1984), 32–44 especially.